# MATERIALISM

# MATERIALISM

## AN OUTLINE OF THE HISTORY OF SCIENTIFIC THOUGHT

BY

M. N. ROY

GYAN

*Published by*

Gyan Publishing House
5, Ansari Road
Daryaganj, New Delhi-110002
Phone: 011-47034999, 9811692060
E-mail: books@gyanbooks.com

*Distribution Network*
gyanbooks.com
India, USA, Canada, UK, Australia



ISBN: 978-93-6280-123-4 (PB)
First Published, 1940

2nd Impression 2024

*Printed at:* Gyan Press, Delhi.



**MATERIALISM**
Author: M. N. ROY

# MATERIALISM

## AN OUTLINE OF THE HISTORY OF SCIENTIFIC THOUGHT

BY

M. N. ROY

# PREFACE

As the sub-title indicates, this book is an outline of the history of scientific thought. It was written originally as the introduction to a larger work which will be published soon under the title "The Philosophical Consequences of Modern Science". What was originally meant to be an introduction, having grown rather too big for that purpose, is being published as an independent book. Nevertheless, it remains a part of the larger book, as its introduction.

It is a general belief among those with a smattering of modern scientific knowledge, mostly derived from the popular writings of physicists like Jeans, Eddington and others, that the discoveries of the twentieth century's physics have exploded Materialism. Certain discoveries of modern physics are, indeed, revolutionary, demanding a thorough revision of some traditional concepts. But no serious philosophical discussion is possible except on the background of a proper appreciation of the fundamental principles of philosophy. Materialism was not the product of the eighteenth and nineteenth centuries. It is as old as philosophy itself. And the history of philosophy is the history of the development of scientific thought. Therefore, a general knowledge of philosophy ever since its very beginning, is essential for an intelligent discussion of the philosophical consequences of modern science. It is hoped that this book will serve that purpose.

M. N. ROY

*Dehra Dun, July* 1940.

# CONTENTS

## ERRATA

| Page | Line | Incorrect | Correct. |
|---|---|---|---|
| 18 | 1 | creatures | preachers |
| 32 | 16 | phenomenon of life is | phenomena of nature are |
| 33 | 21 | nomenon | noumenon |
| 34 | 7 & 8 | which throws human though t in | human thought is caught in |
| 43 | 13 | religious | anti-religious |
| 45 | 11 | mechanistic | materialist |
| 52 | 26 | Maya. | Maya." |
| 53 | 9–10 | Brihadaranyak and Taittiriyak | and Brihadaranyak |
| 84 | 20 | a form of popular form and | a form of |
| 89 | 9 | marked | marks |
| 94 | 10 | gods | supernatural beings |
| 102 | 21 | equal | unequal |
| 115 | 12 | void space, | void, |
| 126 | 13–14 | developed for | were anxious for |
| 142 | 21 | ceased | ceases |
| 142 | Last line | entity | entity, |
| 168 | 21 | the middle ages | the later middle ages. |
| 177 | 22 | with elder | with his elder |
| 180 | 12 | "new philosophy" | "new cosmological conception" |
| 180 | 17 | the materialistic | the co-ordination of the materialistic |

# MATERIALISM

# INTRODUCTION

## THE IDEOLOGY OF ORTHODOX NATIONALISM

THE common characteristic of Indian patriotism, irrespective of its shades, is the antipathy for the "Western civilisation". The degree of this characteristic common complexion of the ideology of Indian nationalism, of course, varies according to the social background of particular political groups. The attitude, for example, of the Hindu Mahasabha or the Arya Samaj, not to mention the die-hard Sanatanists, is of fierce hostility, backed by sanctimonious self-righteousness. On the other end of the front stand the liberal reformers who stultify themselves politically as well as ideologically by disavowing admiration for a course of social development which they must follow, if they are true to their professions and principles.

The realisation of the political ideals of Indian nationalism will clear the obstacles to a capitalist development of the country; India will "civilise" herself on the model of the West. That would be all the more true, if the ideal of national freedom were to be realised under the flag of liberalism; and a purely nationalist political programme is inseparable from that flag.* In order to outgrow the domination of capitalist interest, exercised directly or indirectly, Indian political aspirations must

* This was written in 1938. Since then, the political aspirations of the Congress have been given more concrete form, and to-day they are hardly distinguishable from those of the Liberals.

transcend the narrow limits of orthodox nationalism. The ideal of national freedom must not be circumscribed by petty political aspirations,* and reflect the objective striving of the masses for social liberation. In that case, political power having been captured by the toiling masses, India would be able to inherit the great achievements of the "Western civilisation," free from the abuses of capitalist exploitation, associated with it. Then, and only then, would a critical attitude towards "Western civilisation," *in its entirety*, enrich the ideology of Indian Renaissance. As the situation is, and as the perspective appears at present, all the diatribes against "Western civilisation" are entirely out of place. It is so foolish to sling mud at the moon for its blemishes when you are crying to have it. It is all the worse, not at all complimentary for the intellectual level of a movement, to aspire for something without knowing that it is doing so.

Between the two extremes of frankly professed revivalism and the self-contradictory attitude of the modernist Liberals, there stands the Congress, with millions of heterogeneous adherents and sympathisers, occupying the centre of the nationalist ideological front, under the proud banner of Gandhism. The attitude of the Congress is the most typical and representative. In spite of all its obvious contradictions, mental acrobatics, unexpected somersaults, "Himalayan mistakes" (which in plain language mean woeful debacles), Gandhism still dominates the ideology of the great bulk of the politically awakened and forward moving (though not forward

* The pettiness of the political ideal of the Gandhist Purna Swaraj has now been exposed.

looking) sections of the Indian population. And Gandhism is believed to be the veritable antithesis of Western civilisation.

A Gandhist need no longer decry railways, motor cars and even modern hospitals as Satanic contrivances. The Prophet himself has moved far away from that original position of pristine purity. Close association with not only the Gujarati cotton kings, but also all the modern magnates of money, and honorary membership of the Indian Chamber of Commerce cannot but dampen the zeal against modern industry. Illustrious patrons of the Congress—Birlas, Bajajes and others of their kind—may put on the white cap, but are the last persons to brook any serious opposition to capitalism. Yet, the typical Indian nationalist, inebriated with frothy Gandhism, speaks as the prophet of a new civilisation. To be sure, he does not know what his pet ideal would look like when, if ever, realised. But he very emphatically proclaims that India does not want to imitate the West. If he only knew how ridiculous it is to be heading towards a goal, protesting all the time that he does not want to go to that despised destination!

So unreasonable is this article of faith of Indian nationalism that even people with a more or less decidedly progressive outlook start with the declaration that they are not admirers of Western civilisation whenever they dare criticise the established social customs and institutions. These half-hearted, shame-faced reformers repeat parrot-like the supercilious disapproval of Western civilisation, even when they advocate the introduction of social and political institutions associated with it. For example, give freedom to the women as in Europe and America, but don't let them abandon the ideal of Indian womanhood, don't let them be contaminated by the "abuse" of that freedom, as is the case with the women in the West; abolish the caste system, but guard against the promiscuity of Western society; encourage capitalism, but avoid the greediness of Western materialism; get rid of religious superstitions and have a rationalist view of life, but don't accept experimental science as the only source of human knowledge. Such is the attitude of the advocates of progress, of those who grudgingly admit that there is something wrong with Indian society, and are distressed not to find a remedy in ancient traditions. They find it difficult to reject the outcome of a thousand years of human progress called Western civilisation. Yet, they don't have the courage to break with the old and embrace the new.

Theirs is the theory of the so-called synthesis, a compromise between progress and reaction; the compromise is to take place on the basis of the "spiritual genius" of Indian culture. The abominable Western civilisation will be admitted into Holy India only after it has performed the ceremony of "*Prayaschitta*". The Western civilisation is not altogether rejected; it is only asked to place itself under the purifying influence of India. The spokesmen of this spiritual imperialism do not know what they are talking about. They expound the doctrine of "synthesis" with a show of philosophic wisdom. But what do they actually propose? An impossibility —harmonious inter-weaving of two mutually exclusive systems of culture and forms of thought, belonging to different historical epochs, centuries apart.

Philosophically understood, synthesis is the process of a new positive category coming out of the negation of something which has previously existed also as a positive category. Chemically, synthesis results from what is called a compound mixture. It is something entirely new, and different from the old, and the constituents from which it results. A synthesis of the conflicting elements contained in what is known as Western civilisation, (that is, capitalist society) will be the rise of an entirely new type of civilisation on the basis laid by the capitalist civilisation itself. The positive elements of the capitalist civilisation will go into the making of a higher form of civilisation. Indians talking of a synthesis propose just the reverse process. They suggest that the "good" in Western civilisation should be adopted by India, to be harmonised with her native culture.

Two functions of the capitalist civilisation can be styled "good", if the term is defined as progressive, inducive to human progress. One is destructive: Capitalism performs a "good" function when it disrupts, and eventually clears away, the ruins of the mediaeval feudal social order with its religious mode of thought. The other "good" function of capitalism—the constructive function—is to bring about industrial development to a point from where humanity can easily enter into a higher stage of social evolution. The destructive "good" function of capitalism cannot be harmonised with the traditional Indian culture which was based upon a social order, disrupted and finally destroyed by it more than two hundred years ago in Europe. It is doubtful that the Indian social "synthesists" would welcome that "good" in Western civilisation. To recognise that function of capitalism as good, would mean wholehogging for Western civilisation. Then, there could be no more wise talk of synthesis.

Those who cannot appreciate without reserve the historical value of the destructive "good" function of capitalism, cannot possibly welcome and avail of its constructive "good",—its positive outcome. Moreover, the latter "good" function opens up a vista of the future which is entirely irreconcilable with a wistful look backwards.

Indian nationalist criticism of the capitalist civilisation is not directed against its real evil—the reactionary, degrading, degenerating features it develops in the period of decay. Indian nationalists reject precisely what is "good" in capitalist civilisation. Culturally, the positive outcome of the capitalist civilisation has been the tremendous advance of science, in theory and practice—an advance which has prepared the ground for final liberation of man from the age-long spiritual bondage.

The basic evil of capitalist civilisation, in the cultural aspect, has been the systematic and persistent attempt to block the spiritual liberation of man, even when it was creating the conditions favourable for that liberation. That was done by protecting and fostering religion (of course, in modernised forms), idealist philosophy and all sorts of the associated obscurantist metaphysical speculation, just when the triumphal march of scientific knowledge was disrupting the foundation of these relics of the dark ages. Yet, curiously enough, materialism is held, by the Indian nationalists, to be the fundamental sin of Western civilisation!

As a matter of fact, the situation is just the reverse: Materialist philosophy is a bugbear no less hated and combated by the ruling classes of the West than by our nationalists—the would-be rulers of India. Why? Because materialist philosophy is the mighty instrument for the spiritual liberation of mnkind. This weapon, originally hammered out roughly by the great thinkers of antiquity (India had her share of that glorious pioneering work), has been perfected in course of the history of capitalist culture. Therefore, all fighters for freedom and honest advocates of progress must appreciate Western civilisation as the hitherto most brilliant chapter of human history. To decry that imposing monument of human progress, from the standpoint of an antiquated culture, as the Indian nationalists do, is simply reactionary.

"Western civilisation is materialist" and "Eastern culture is spiritual"—these are the favourite shibboleths of the Indian nationalist ideology. While harping on this theme *ad nauseum*, none takes the pain of proving the contention. It is regarded simply as an axiomatic truth, which becomes all the more categorial, the more it is asserted dogmatically, and proclaimed loudly. The purpose of this book is not controversial. It will nevertheless be demonstrated that, what is claimed to be the "special genius" of Indian culture, is not special at all; that spiritualism, that is, the religious form of thought, characterises human ideology everywhere in a certain stage of social evolution.* It will also be shown that the modes of thought change in accordance with the variation of social environments, and therefore no particular way of thinking can be the eternal and immutable characteristic of any people.

If India clings tenaciously to a particular mode of thought which has been rejected or reformed or camouflaged by the Western nations, it is not because the latter are morally depraved by nature, and therefore have not been able to remain on the high level of a religious ideology. It simply proves that advance of civilisation (progressive conquest of nature by man) has enabled those nations to think more in terms of reason and positive knowledge than in terms of faith and metaphysical fantasies. It simply proves that changes in the conditions of life inevitably revolutionise human ideology. It proves that India clings to an antiquated mode of thought because she did not experience similar changes. Otherwise, the people of India also would to-day be thinking more or less similarly as the Western peoples. They did so until only three hundred years ago.

The gigantic transformation of the conditions of life experienced by the Western peoples during the last two hundred years has created the gulf which separates them ideologically from the Indian people. Subject India to the same process of transformation, and the gulf will close up in no time.

* The history of Western Spiritualism, a chapter in the larger book of which the present one is an introduction, may be published, pending the publication of the latter, under the name "Western Spiritualism."

The great bulk of Indian nationalists exclaim: "Ah! That is precisely what we want to avoid"; and complacently believe to have proved the spiritual superiority of the Indian culture. Is not the desire itself born of an innate spiritual inclination? Unless Indians were by nature spiritually inclined, how could they resist the temptation of travelling the road of greed and worldly grandeur like the wayward peoples of the West? But one may ask an entirely different question: Was it by choice that India did not travel that road. Is she resisting the temptation even to-day, The least regard for the facts of history and the realities of the present situation will compel the answer to be decisively in the negative. Even the disappointed jackal makes a laughing-stock of itself by attempting to hide the chagrin in an ill-fitting garb of lofty indifference for the sour grapes. Such harmful self-deception should not have any place in the ideology of a great people in the process of a renaissance.

The proclamation that India wishes to avoid travelling the path of Western nations implies two very important admissions. Firstly, that, given the similar changes in their conditions of life, the Indian people also would think just in the same way as the peoples of the West. This admission knocks the bottom off the dogma of innate spirituality of the Indians. It is admitted that India has remained wedded to the religious mode of thought simply because she has had no opportunity for outgrowing it. The second admission is that Indian nationalism is utterly futile. It does not believe in its own programme. The nationalist movement, the striving for political freedom, itself is the decisive testimony to the fact that the Indian people are just as much concerned with the conditions of life as others.

Political freedom will enable the Indian people to catch up with the progress of two hundred years that separates them from the Western nations. The historical significance of Indian nationalism is precisely the realisation of that which its prevalent ideology disclaims! Is it not a pitiful spectacle, If you really believe that you are spiritually superior to others, that your superiority is innate, then why bother about other things of life, Being innate, your spiritual genius cannot be destroyed or corrupted by the vicissitudes of the mundane existence. So, your nationalism is a mistake; the will to political freedom is a deviation from your spiritual nature. Show your spirituality by bearing the cross of political slavery and economic ruin. Either your spirituality is a sham, or your nationalism is a huge joke.

Then, to hark back to history and a legend is a double-edged sword. It cuts both ways. The West, too, can boast of its Janakas, and they are living to-day, giving a spiritualist complexion to the materialist civilisation. If acquisition of wealth is justified, provided that it is devoted to good purposes, can you accuse a Rockfeller of materialism? Does he not spend huge sums for the very virtuous purpose of spreading Christianity, for saving millions and millions of heathen souls? Has not a Carnegie contributed magnificently to the promotion of peace? The list can be prolonged to include practically all the richest men of America and

Europe. Yet, those are the very people who impersonate what is decried as Western materialism.

A dispassionate observation of facts unmistakably reveals the essential similarly of the ideals and activities pursued in the daily life of all peoples irrespective of the geographical location of their habitats. The apparent diversity is only a form. The great bulk of the Indian people are also concerned mainly with the material things of life. Not for enjoyment, but as a matter of necessity. It is not only the case to-day, it has been so always. And the culture of a people, after all, is to be judged by the standard of its bulk. High-sounding phrases or pet doctrines, invented by the "intellectual elite", do not reflect the real ideology of a people. Even intellectuals themselves, in practical life, are obliged to come down from the giddy altitude of their ideals. The great majority of Indian intellectuals are ardent believers in the spiritual superiority of their race. They are eloquent defenders of the "Aryan" ideals of life. They are convinced, by some queer and questionable process of reasoning, that such noble qualities as the spirit of sacrifice, sincerity, purity of mind, etc., are Indian monopolies. They cherish the day-dream of participating in the mission of India to save the tormented humanity from the sin of materialism. This all sounds so beautiful, and it is so exhilarating to repeat it with a ring of conviction. But what, after all this moonshine, is the ideal the Indian intellectuals actually pursue? To get a semblance of education, not for the sake of education, but for its market value; to equip themselves with the object of acquiring worldly goods. Do the youth of the materialist West pursue any different ideal?

If the concern for the physical necessities of life is "materialism", the peoples of the West are no more to be blamed than the Indian for performing what is only a biological function. No rational person can ever dispute the fact that to subsist and reproduce are the essential functions of every organism. The human being naturally tries to perform these basic biological functions unde rthe most favourable conditions. The ability to create such conditions, and to improve them progressively, separates man from the lower animals; that is to say, hankering for comfort is a biological urge. Anyone who would dispute the view, must defend the absurd proposition that the cave-dweller is the ideal human being.

But the opponents of materialism, of course, do not stretch their spiritualism to such an obviously absurd extent, although logically they should. Because, who is to determine where the line is to be drawn? Once the biological necessity is admitted, any limit to it can be set only arbitrarily. In spite of all humbug, there is scriptural evidence that materialism, in the sense of the desire to subsist, reproduce and acquire worldly goods, is not against the genius of Indian culture. According to the scriptures, the object of human life is fourfold: *Dharma*, *Artha*, *Kama* and *Moksha*. Sandwiched piously in between *Dharma* and *Moksha*, *Artha* and *Kama* do not cease to mean what they are. The fact remains that the acquisition of worldly goods as well as sexual enjoyment was not only sanctioned scripturally, but was recognised as the object of human life, on equal footing with religion and salvation. Enjoyment in general is the broad interpretation of the term *Kama* given by all the commentators.

The Mahabharat contains the most elaborate and comprehensive exposition of *Dharma*. The closing verse of the Epic declares: "*Artha* and *Kama* are derived from *Dharma*." This very significant declaration is put in the mouth of Vyasa. The divine inspiration of that saintly law-giver of ancient India was the sanction for the codes of *Dharma* formulated in the Mahabharat. The injuction is: Be religious, and you will have all the pleasures of the world. The materialistic essence of Indian spiritualism is evident. What is still more significant is that the saintly injunction is associated with a note of exasperation: "But none listens to me." In the very "Golden Age" of Indian history the pursuit of *Artha* and *Kama* was not even restricted by *Dharma*. The prevalent "materialism" must have exasperated the saintly law-giver.

One of the charges commonly hurled against the Western civilisation is that of sexuality. On this point again, Indian sanctimoniousness is borne out neither by present practice nor by past theories. In fact, ancient and mediaeval literature of no other country is so full of erotics as that of India. Leave aside the classical example of the mediaeval Vaishnava and the ancient Bhagavata cults; the Brahma Sutras themselves lay down: "The sexual instinct is germinal in the child, and obtains full expression when the proper age comes. So...."

It is not at all difficult to reconstruct the conclusion left unsaid. It must be, since sex is a natural instinct, it is to be enjoyed; the *Dharma* sanctions it. According to the Gita also, God operates as "the rightful desire (*Kama*) in all creatures." Rightful —that is, according to *Dharma*. But in spite of such an admirably liberal interpretation, *Dharma* was superceded by the other ideals of human life even in the Golden Age of Indian history.

At the end of the Mahabharat, Vyasa informs that *Dharma* was generally disregarded. *Dharma* evidently meant social codes which, in a backward stage of human development, are defined everywhere in religious terms, and remain in operation on the authority of some divine or heavenly sanctions. One must acquire worldly goods, satisfy the sexual urge, and enjoy the pleasure of physical life generally, but under certain conditions—governed by the laws of the established society.

Does the daily life in the materialist West fall short of this ideal? None but a raving maniac, utterly ignorant of the subject under discussion, would venture an answer in the affirmative. Highway robbery as a means of acquiring wealth and the caveman's method of winning his mate are no more practised in the Western countries than in India. The peoples of Europe and America pursue the objects of *Artha* and *Kama* just as much governed by *Dharma* as the Indians. And essentially, there is little difference in what they respectively accept as the legitimate limitations to their pursuits. In the last analysis, the limitations, be they in the form of the Hindu Samhitas or generally accepted moral codes or the civil law, can be reduced to the good old Mosaic Ten Commandments.

As regards the fourth object, *Moksha*, the average European or American is a Christian, and is as true to his religious belief as the average Indian is to his. It is simply impertinent to maintain that the average Westerner is hypocritical about his religious beliefs, whereas the average Indian is sincere. There is absolutely no evidence in support of this amazing contention, so often made light-heartedly. Salvation of the soul is a cardinal principle also of Christianity, and an average European or American Christian, by virtue of being better educated, is able to follow his faith more intelligently than the average Indian whose religion is but a bundle of superstitions and habits. *Moksha* has practically vanished from the latter's religious vision. The struggle for the bare physical existence cruelly governs his whole being, with *Kama*, often in very unappetising forms, dominating the dark corners. Shackles of antiquated social codes, such as the caste regulations together with the civil laws of the British Government, have taken the place of *Dharma*,—the limitation of the pursuit of the two basic objects of human life.

The more reasonable protagonist of spiritualism would come forward with the rejoinder: Granted that the above picture depicts the reality of the situation, it only proves a certain degree of degeneration of our culture; the object of Indian nationalism is to arrest the deplorable process, and revive our spiritual culture as the model for the world. The present failing to prove the case, the evidence for the spiritual superiority of Indian culture is to be discovered in the past. Before *Dharma* degenerated under the impact of Western materialism, *Moksha* shone as the guiding star of life, and *Artha* and *Kama* occupied but minor places in the life of the Hindu. That is the contention. Historically, it is simply not true. Even the legends of the Epics, unscientifically accorded the dignity of history, do not corroborate the contention. The best traditions of Indian culture go back to the beef-eating and soma-drinking Brahmins of the Vedic age. The Epics are full of descriptions of royal courts vying with each other as regards grandeur, luxury and vain glory. Even when *Dharma* was pure, and *Moksha* did not vanish from the vision of life, *Artha* and *Kama* were not despised. They were certainly enjoyed, if not actually worshipped. But you do worship what you enjoy, if worship has any meaning. The quintessence of the *Dharma* of India in her Golden Age is contained in the Santi Parva of the Mahabharat. Read it to find how eager even the Brahmins were to acquire worldly goods.

If the talk of a few is to be taken for the evidence about an entire community, then Europe and specially America deserve the palm of spirituality on the strength of the army of priests vociferously preaching Christian virtues from numerous pulpits. And Christian virtues have no reason to be ashamed before the "Aryan" ideals of life. It would be staking an absurd claim to contend that similar conceptions of God, soul and other spiritual categories might have greater regenerating values when stated in the Indian scriptures. It would be equally illogical and damaging for the very doctrine of spirituality to assert that Christianity was corrupted by materialism, whereas extra-mundane notions of life proved immune to such degeneration in India. If spiritual categories are what they are claimed to be, they must be incorruptible under all circumstances and everywhere. But if they lose force in one place, and under one set of circumstances, their immutability is disproved, and it is but a logical deduction that, given similar change of conditions, they would go the same way everywhere.

"What does it profit a man if he gains the whole world and loses his soul?" This highly spiritualistic sermon is repeated every day throughout the Christian world. As a matter of fact, Christianity contains all the articles of faith, all the metaphysical doctrines and moral dogmas which are cited as the evidence of the spiritual nature of Indian culture. Christ himself taught: "The kingdom of God is within you." It means that the salvation of man is to be attained through the realisation of the soul—an ideal identical with the "Atmadarshan" of the Hindus. St. Paul chided his audience: "Are Ye so foolish? Having begun in spirit, are you made perfect by the flesh?" Coming to the fathers of the Church, we find Gregory of Nicea teaching: "Human soul is identical with God." Finally, one may learn from the greatest Christian theologian, Thomas Aquinas: "That intellectual light that is within us, is not else than a certain participated likeness of the Uncreated Light in which are contained the Eternal Reasons."

No use murmuring adverse reflections or entertaining doubts about the divinity of the creatures of the Christian Gospel or about the sincerity of the faith of their congregations. On this issue the table can be turned against the Indians just as well. The divinity of the Brahman, the standard-bearer of "Aryan" culture, is palpably open to doubt. The modern Swami can hardly claim superiority to an up-to-date Christian theologian. Only blind prejudice and impotent national chauvinism can brand the Christian congregations of Europe and America with spiritual inferiority to the Indian masses. The former have at least a faith, whereas the latter have only superstitions. There is absolutely no reason to believe that, when one repeats the enigmatic aphorisms of Vedanta, or recites the Gita, his catholicity is beyond doubt, whereas the sincerity of a Christian priest is to be suspected when he teaches the Gospel of Christ.

There are those who identify materialism with capitalism. They cannot denounce materialism as a Western product. Capitalism is not a thing of to-day. Nor did it drop from heaven or spring out of the hell. It is an economic system which evolved, over a whole period of history. Although, for many reasons, it happened to flourish more luxuriantly in Europe, its germs had been sprouting for hundreds of years in all the civilised countries. The facts, proudly cited, often exaggeratedly, by nationalist historians, regarding the growth of industry (handicraft) and expansion of trade in India, "when the fore-fathers of modern Europe were going naked", only prove that India was heading towards "materialism" even before the European peoples outgrew their primitive innocence. The growth of handicraft and the consequent expansion of trade eventually usher in capitalism. Leaving aside the controversial facts about the pre-historic and antique periods, it can be established with reliable data that commodity production on the basis of handicraft was well advanced in India even before the advent of the Europeans. So, India stood on the threshold of modern capitalism, and was walking into the corrupting embrace of materialism, when Europe was still largely merged in the darkness of the highly "spiritual" middle-ages. Two very important things are thus proved: Firstly, the love of lucre, as typified in capitalism, is not a peculiar feature of Western civilisation; and secondly, India developed this sinful love earlier than Europe.

The Indian nationalist is not ashamed of this sinful love. He only wishes to legalise, rather sanctify, it in a happy and a harmonious wedlock between capital and labour, thereby setting an object lesson to the materialist West. The proposition is to "spiritualise" capitalism. The least understanding of the nature of capitalism would show the absurdity of this utopia. Accumulation of wealth in the possession of the owners of the means of production by exploiting the labour power of the wage-slaves, is the essence of capitalism. That is "greed", if a moral term is to be used for describing a social impulse. The utopia of an ethical capitalism, however, is nothing new. It is an old song. It was heard in the materialist West, long before Gandhi fascinated with it his uncritical followers. The most remarkable thing is that people, passing sweeping judgment against Western civilisation, are often totally ignorant of its history. Some knowledge of the social history of Europe opens one's eyes to the fact that it was the classical home of capitalism, namely, England, which gave birth also to a whole variety of utopian doctrines for the moral rehabilitation of that "unnecessary social evil."

The Christian Socialism of Charles Kingsley and his followers anticipated Gandhism by more than half a century. If William Lovett, the leader of the "moral force" wing of the Chartist movement, was here to-day, he would be found eminently qualified, in every respect, for admission into the inner conclave of the Pope of Indian nationalism, and membership of the Working Committee of the Congress. The Christian Socialists held that disregard for "spiritual values" made the workers bitter against the employers. They set about to "spiritualise" the atmosphere, so that a perfect social harmony could be established for the benefit and happiness of all. To the workers, brutally exploited by rapacious capitalism, and bloodily suppressed by the Government whenever they revolted against intolerable conditions, Kingsley piously preached: "Be fit to be free, and God Himself will set you free.... There will be no true freedom without virtue, no true science without religion, no true industry without the fear of God and love to your fellow-citizen." It may be pertinently pointed out that the Gospel of Christ, as falsified by Saint Matthew, was the source of inspiration of Kingsley's highly "spiritualist" view of freedom. (The original Gospel recorded by St. Luke was a powerful cry of revolt. Christianity rose as the ideology of the rebellious slaves. As such, originally it was as sublime as any religion can ever be.) Kingsley's sermon to the toiling masses, bleeding on the cross of capitalism, was of course livened up, and made more attractive by denunciation of the rich with an apostolic fervour. But that was followed by the very pragmatic proposition to throw some crumbs of justice and magnanimity to the hungry multitude before it was too late to stem the ominous tide of revolt. The purpose of the Christian Socialist propaganda—of Kingsley, Maurice, Stephens and other devout reformers—was to divert the attention of the victims of capitalist greed from the sorrows and sufferings of life to illusive spiritual and moral ideals. The hero of Kingsley's novel, Anton Locke, is an ex-Chartist workman. The philosophy of deception is put into his mouth: "Fool that I was! It was within rather than without that I should reform. For my part, I seem to have learned that the only thing to regulate the world is not more of any system, good or bad, but simply more of the spirit of God."

One of the master-builders of the British Empire, Disraeli, came under the wholesome influence of Christian Socialism. He bitterly criticised the laissez-faire policy of the whig bourgeoisie as the cause of the social misery, depicted with real artistic merit in his famous book "Sybil", and advocated social reform—a benevolent attitude to the working class. Does the pious "anti-capitalism of the Gandhists propose anything more spiritual?

Another famous British statesman of the nineteenth century, Sir Robert Peel, said: "Take my word for it, it is not prudent to trust yourself to a man who does not believe in God, and in a future life after death." As a matter of fact, all the leading men of the nineteenth century—the classical age of vulgar materialism running rampant—were all highly religious, God-fearing souls. Philosophical materialism of the eighteenth century—of the French Encyclopedists—had turned out to be dangerous for the established order of society. So, the ruling class had taken refuge under the protection of God, and their pious spokesmen agitated for more benevolence, more kindness, more justice, in the relations of the established social order based on the exploitation of man by man.

The United States of America is generally considered to be the greatest and most hardened sinner. The object of the "National Recovery Policy" of President Roosevelt was defined by General Hugh S. Johnson as follows: "To see that capital gets a decent return, and at the same time to make sure that labour gets a more generous share of the profits." Who would assert that this is not the conception of a humane and just economic system that the Indian nationalists propose to build up as an improvement upon the materialist capitalism of the West? What is the spiritual-idealistic principle underlying this noble conception? Not to kill the goose that lays the golden eggs. Not to be so greedy as to hack down the branch on which you are sitting. See your picture in others; hear your voice echoed by others, and you will know yourself.

Yet another example: "Thou shalt not make mammon thy god; thou shalt not make gold thy god, but thy servant; that shalt not suffer the paradox of poverty and plenty, else thou sinnest grievously." Who do you think pronounced those biblical words? An Assistant Secretary of State of the United States of America under the Roosevelt regime. This Mahatmic sermon could be preached just as well by any orthodox Indian nationalist. But in practice, the cap is not placed, neither in India nor in the West, on the head it fits, The hypocritical sermon is meant for the masses, so that the preserves of the fortunate few are not in the least touched. The sanctimonious attitude towards poverty is not born of spiritualism, but of the fear of revolution. It is highly interesting to note that the object of the rulers of the most materialist country of the West happens to be identical with the Gandhist attitude towards capitalism. Gandhi also denounces capitalism, but does not advocate its abolition. His doctrine of non-violence precludes any such revolutionary programme. His avowed desire is to establish harmonious relations between the capitalists and workers—to persuade the former to be benevolent guardians of the latter. Addressing a public meeting at Nagpur in November 1933, the Mahatma declared: "I have been doing my very best to secure adequate wages for the labourers and to convert the capitalists to be the trustees of workers rather than their employers." On innumerable occasions, previous to that and subsequently, he has repeated the same sentiment. In the light of such utterances, the Mahatma cannot be looked upon as a greater enemy of capitalism than Disraeli. Both advocate giving the bitter pill a sugar-coating.

The Christian Socialism of Kingsley and others simply aided capitalism which it proposed to reform. Anton Locke's pious pessimism captured the depressed spirit of the workers, heavily defeated in their first great struggle for freedom. A few miserable crumbs from the overflowing table of the capitalists, accompanied by the expression of pious wishes, succeeded in making the workers accept wage-slavery as a normal condition of life. The masses were brought back under the spell of religiosity, and meekly submitted to the established codes of ethics and law. The average English worker became not only a believer in constitutional reform, but also a devoutly religious man.

In no other country is to be found a community of civilised men and women more religious than the English proletariat. Since the doctrine of spiritualism bore them such magnificent fruits, the English capitalists also became converts to it, conveniently forgetting the rationalist and materialist traditions of their revolutionary forefathers. Sickening philistinism ran rampant in the land of Bacon, Hobbes and Locke. The Victorian era—the period of phenomenal capitalist development and colonial expansion—was intensely religious. Gladstonian liberalism sailed merrily with the fraudulent colours of harmony between capital and labour.

No reasonable person can possibly believe that the magic wand of Gandhism will spiritualise the capitalist system in any different fashion. It is not a part of the "spiritual genius" of India to abolish capitalism. The proposition is only to "moralise" it, humanise it. Materialism, in the worst sense of the term, always thrives in the *Gairic* garb of spiritualism. Those who reject spiritualism, that is, religious mode of thought, have nothing but disdain for what is vulgarly called materialism. Their moral attitude is depicted in the words of Epicurus —one of the illustrious founders of philosophical materialism. He cast away the belief in gods and threw off the shackles of religion, not to "eat, drink and be merry", but "in order to be noble and virtuous because it is a pleasure to be so". The vulgar doctrine of "eat, drink and be merry", maliciously attributed to the materialist sage of ancient Greece by the barbarous Christian theologians, has been adopted by the ruling classes which devoutly profess Christian virtues, and pompously talk of high ideals. Nor is vulgar materialism confined to the ruling classes of the West. It has been practised by them also in India in the past and is practised at present as well. The Epics and other classical literature are full of incontestable evidence to that effect. At present, the orthodox cotton kings of Ahmedabad, for example, do not lead a life more altruistic than the westernised Parsi mill-owners of Bombay. The Banya who washes his corpulent frame daily in the holy water of the Ganges and spends several hours in Puja-patha, beats Shylock in his game. It is just as erroneous to castigate the entire Western world for the vulgar materialism of its ruling class, as it is to declare Indian culture innately spiritual on the strength of the reactionary orthodoxy of the few having a stake in the established order of things. The multitude of people, in the West as well as in the East, are simply engrossed in the performance of biological functions. The desire to eat, drink and be merry, on the part of those, who at best can ever get just a glimpse of that kingdom of heaven, is a veritable incentive to progress,—an urge to freedom, spiritual as well as mundane. Spiritualism, discouraging this legitimate desire in them, stands in the way not only of material progress, but of the real spiritual emancipation of mankind.

The antithesis of spiritualism is *philosophical* materialism which has absolutely nothing to do with the vulgar characterisation "eat, drink and be merry". It is not the ideology of the capitalist Western civilisation. On the contrary, all the intellectual forces of the capitalist society are concentrated in fighting the hated and dreaded foe—the philosophy of revolution which heralds a civilisation higher than the capitalist. So, by denouncing materialism, the Indian nationalists do not reject the capitalist civilisation, but enter into an unholy alliance with it. They place themselves in such a position because of their erroneous notion about materialism. This does not mean that a better acquaintance with the enemy would make them love it. But in that case, they would at least be able to talk more intelligently and seriously. At the same time, there would be a differentiation in their ranks. The progressive elements, freed from the prejudice born of ignorance, might find in philosophical materialism a powerful means for the realisation of their goal. In any case, they are bound to break away from the traditions of religious orthodoxy.

To-day, in the Western countries, the bourgeoisie are carrying on desperately a losing struggle against the revolutionary philosophy of materialism; but their forefathers had to carry on the historic fight against the religiosity of mediaeval barbarism in order to shake the moral and spiritual foundation of the pre-capitalist society. Their ideological weapon in that fight was philosophical materialism. The revolutionary weapon, forged originally by the great thinkers of antiquity, was profitably employed and greatly sharpened in course of the struggle of the rising bourgeoisie.

Materialist philosophy has to be called in to assist at the re-birth also of India. As long as the progressively minded intellectuals will remain wedded to the antiquated forms of religious thought, superficially rationalised to be all the more harmful, because of its deceptiveness, they will simply stultify themselves. The boldness required for tearing down the rotten structure of Indian society, in the vicious atmosphere of which all incentive to progress is chocked, can be born only out of a spirit set free by scientific knowledge.

The weakness of Indian nationalism lies in its ideology. An objectively progressive movement is saddled with a whole cargo of reactionary ideas which contradict its very being. The result is the puzzling sight of Goliath whipped by David. The latent forces of the movement are being cramped by its ideology. If we want to go forward in the future, we must have the courage to break away from the past. The longer we linger with the virtues of the past, virtues which have ceased to be virtues, having become veritable vices in course of time, the farther shall we remain from the victories of the future. The nationalists who want to go forward must seek inspiration in philosophical materialism which alone can make a correct appreciation of the past culture as containing the germs for a superior culture to come. Only that much in past greatness is useful which helps to attain a greater future. The rest of the past are shackles to be shaken by those who want to be free and go ahead. Therefore, a correct understanding of philosophical materialism is an urgent necessity of the moment. It will immensely strengthen the forces of progress, and hasten the much delayed renaissance of India. On the other hand, it will enable our opponents, that is, the ideologists of reaction, slavery, degeneration and degradation, to put up their case with a modicum of philosophical knowledge, so that some intellectual pleasure might be derived from fighting them.

In order to make the issues clear, it is necessary to set aside catch-phrases and empty shiboleths. The fight between spiritualism and materialism is a philosophical controversy. It cannot be carried on fruitfully with wrong notions by those ignorant of the issues involved and parties implicated. A philosophical controversy, involving the basic categories of thought and fundamental values of human culture must be carried on a philosophical plane. There must be clear definitions, systematic reasoning, and correct methods. The entire cultural history of mankind is the armoury from which weapons are to be brought out. The object of this book is to prepare the ground for such an ideological fight.

Having indicated the important fact, confused by meaningless phrases and flashy shiboleths, that human desires, behaviours and actions, sanctimoniously, but erroneously condemned as materialism, are biological functions constituting the very essence of life, which differentiates the organic world from the inanimate nature, it now remains for these introductory remarks to state briefly the real issue of the age-long fight between materialism and spiritualism, knowledge and faith, science and religion. Should biological functions be denounced as vices, corrupting or eclipsing the spiritual essence of man, India, past or present, could not be absolved from the ridiculous charge any more than the West. The Western capitalist civilisation detests materialism no less heartily, and combats it with no less determination, than the defenders of the spiritualist culture of India. The only difference is that, while the former carries on the struggle intelligently, fully acquainted with the nature of the foe, the latter, in their ignorance, confound the friend with the foe, and pathetically fall foul of their own ideal.

Philosophical materialism, though evolved by the illustrious fathers and forefathers of modern Western civilisation, is no longer its ideology. Western civilisation has rejected philosophical materialism, and to-day fights it tooth and nail, not because it has decided to atone for the sins of its forefathers. Philosophical materialism is the message of freedom. Spiritualism, that is, religion in all its forms and the idealist philosophy, is the ideology of a class-ridden society; it is a mighty weapon in the hands of the ruling class to defend their position of power and privilege. The philosophy of the Western ruling class is also essentially spiritualist. Its kinship with what is called the special genius of Indian culture is very close. When that is perceived, the absurdity of the sanctimonious hostility to Western materialism becomes evident. The pious prophets of India's spiritual mission stand out in their native colour, as defenders of the cult of the ruling class, and avowed enemies of the philosophy of freedom.

An exposition of the basic principles of the materialist philosophy, and the broad outlines of the history of its development, will make the contrast between the two opposing forms of thought clear. The issue will thus stand out in a clear relief. A concise definition will dispel the erroneous notion of materialism prevalent in India, and will serve as the standard to judge the real nature of the dominating ideology of the capitalist Western civilisation. Thus measured methodically, instead of being approached with preconceived notions, the governing ideology of the Western capitalist civilisation will be found to be philosophically as non-materialistic as the Indian culture. Conversely, it will be found to be logical to draw the conclusion that Indian spiritualism, on its part, must also have a materialist content. To discover the background of reality behind the thick fog of fiction, will then clearly be the urgent task of the ideologists of Indian Renaissance. Such a correct appreciation of the cultural aspects of Western civilisation, simultaneously with a critical view of Indian traditions, will put an end to the habit of estimating the value of human culture by the points of compass. Such a critical comparative study will do away with the imaginary gulf between the East and the West. It will reduce the supposed absolute difference between the two groups of mankind to a matter of mere distance in time. The qualitative will be brought down to the plane of the quantitative. It will be seen that the peoples of the East and of the West do not live respectively in two different worlds, governed by two different sets of laws, having two different standards of value; that they simply belong to two stages of social evolution, and their difference is no more absolute than that between two historical periods in the process of human development.

# CHAPTER I

## PHILOSOPHY AND METAPHYSICS

THE ignorance of the primitive man imagines super-natural forces behind natural phenomena. But his mental development being too backward to think in the abstract, he conceives the imaginary super-natural forces as gods, more or less like himself, only with immensely greater powers. Yet, he is not capable of conceiving beings as essentially superior to himself. The gods, therefore, are more or less like human beings with similar physical construction, analogous feelings and passions. In every respect, they are only idealised human beings, representing the picture of what the primitive man would himself like to be.

These fantasies, however, do not satisfy those who want to know why things happen as they do. The phenomenon of life is not explained by the childish conception of a god holding out a lamp from behind the clouds, or the poetic conception of the sun-god riding in his chariot from the east to the west. Nursery tales may amuse a grown-up man, but do not convince him. Imagination is not explanation; fantasy is not knowledge. To explain nature is the function of philosophy. Speculation about the causes of natural phenomena begins as soon as man reaches an intellectual level where his spiritual needs are no longer satisfied by the superstitions and fantasies of natural religion.

Philosophy, as defined by Pythagoras, is "contemplation, study and knowledge of the nature." Its function is to know things as they are, and to find the common origin of the diverse phenomena of nature, in nature itself. In the earlier stages of its development, philosophy, by its very nature, was materialistic. Later on, its dignity and distinction were monopolised by metaphysical and speculative thought. Philosophy begins when man's spiritual needs are no longer satisfied by the primitive natural religion which imagines and worships a variety of gods as personifications of the diverse phenomena of nature. The grown-up man discredits the nursery-tales, with which he was impressed in his spiritual childhood and might still be amused. Intellectual growth impels and emboldens him to seek in nature itself the causes of all natural phenomena; to find in nature a unity behind its diversity.

Metaphysics also begins with the desire to discover a unity behind the diversity. But it leaves the ground of philosophy in quest of a nomenon above and beyond nature, something which is distinct from the phenomena. Thus, it abandons the enquiry into what really exists with the object of acquiring knowledge about it, and plunges into the wilderness of speculation. It takes up the absurd task of knowing the intangible as the condition for the knowledge of the tangible. Speculative philosophy is the attempt to explain the concrete realities of existence in the light of a hypothetical absolute. It is the way not to truth, but to dream; not to knowledge but to illusion. Instead of trying to understand the world, the only reality given to man, speculative philosophy ends in denying the existence of the only reality and in declaring it to be a figment of man's imagination. An enquiry which denies the very existence of the object to be enquired, is bound to end in idle dreams and hopeless confusion. The conception of a creator or the prejudice about a Supreme Being, First Principle, Final Cause, leads to teleology, which throws human thought in the vicious circle of metaphysics which for such a long time has appropriated the distinction of philosophy.

If the enquiry about the origin of the Universe starts not from the *terra incognita* of the hypothetical First Principle, but from the tangible and knowable concrete, it reveals the eternalness of nature, having no place for a creator. The assumption of a nomenon behind the world of phenomena, of an absolute reality behind deceptive appearances, is not the simple and right course. Speculative philosophy, therefore, beats about the bush without ever coming out of the confusion of its own creation. It is, as Feuerbach depicted, "like a hungry animal running round and round on a waste, as if driven by an evil spirit, while all around there lies endless green field."

Strictly speaking, philosophy is materialism, and materialism is the only possible philosophy. For, it represents the knowledge of nature as it really exists—knowledge acquired through the contemplation, observation and investigation of the phenomena of nature itself. Therefore, materialism is not the monstrosity it is generally supposed to be. It is not the cult of "eat, drink and be merry", as it has been depicted by its ignorant or malicious adversaries. It simply maintains that the origin of everything that really exists is matter; that there does not exist anything but matter, all other appearances being transformations of matter, and these transformations are governed necessarily by mechanical laws inherent in nature.

With the assumption that the phenomena of nature are determined by the will of some super-natural being or beings, philosophy must make room for faith. What is super-natural, must be always beyond the ken of the knowledge of man, himself a product of nature, and therefore limited by the laws of nature. As soon as the cause of the phenomenal world is thus placed beyond the realm of human knowledge, the world itself becomes incomprehensible. There is the end of philosophy. Man must not aspire to solve the problems of the Universe. He should simply believe that the world is so because the god or the gods have made it so. It is idle to ask why god has made it so, and whence did god himself come. Such questions cannot be answered. Attempts to explain what is inexplicable by its very nature, are mere self-deception. Metaphysics has been very pertinently characterised as a relapse into the savage ideology of magic. "Metaphysicians maintain (as if reverting to the original savage idea) that spirit is the true substance of material things, at least that material things depend upon a spirit or spirits for their existence......In writing about magic, I have indicated the origin of the notion of force...... It appears that these celebrated abstractions, 'force and matter', 'form and substance', 'spirit and body', may be traced back to the savage mind."* Magic practised by the savage, is based upon the belief in invisible, intangible and inscrutable forces which operate from distance without any medium. In the last analysis, the fundamental principle of metaphysics is the same as the belief of the savage.

The difference between metaphysics and materialism is that, while the former starts from an assumption, the latter insists upon dealing with concrete things; while the former is bound by an unverifiable hypothesis and by axioms deduced therefrom, the latter does not accept any hypothesis or axiom unless it can be verified by empirical knowledge. The philosophy which has for its absolute standard an unknown and unknowable entity, and pretends to penetrate the region of the unknown without the help of, and indeed by rejecting, the empirical knowledge of the tangible, is futile speculation. Its "abstract truth" is an empty dream and vain imagination. To seek the knowledge of the phenomena of nature in a hypothetical super-natural nomenon, is logically absurd and philosophically inadmissible. What is itself unexplained, cannot possibly explain other things. Such explanation is not philosophy. It is blind faith—the greatest obstacle to real knowledge. It is a plunge into what Kant so aptly described as the "wide and stormy ocean, the true home of mirage."

Metaphysics pretends to judge the reality of things by a standard, the very existence of which is not proved, and cannot be proved. That is not the

* C. Read, Professor Emeritus, London University, "Man and his Superstitions".

way to the knowledge of things as they are. The correct method is to penetrate the unknown through the way already known. The unknown, if it really exists, must be only a prolongation of the known; it is conceivable only in that sense. Otherwise, if it is something qualitatively different from the known and knowable things, it can never be known. Its existence, therefore, cannot be proved. It is only a fantasy. The chase after a phantom does not increase our knowledge of the reality.

The unknown and invisible unity of the origin of things is but the abstract generalisation of the known and visible particulars. True philosophy was born with this principle. The Ioinan Greek thinkers were the first to attempt a physical explanation of the phenomena of nature; to seek the unity behind the diversity of these phenomena, in nature itself. Those fathers of philosophy were necessarily materialists. The materialism of the ancient philosophers was no more a perverse deviation of sinful men from the pure pursuit of spirit than is modern materialism of experimental science.

As soon as the thinkers of antiquity outgrew the awe for the imposing phenomena of nature, they became curious about their causes. That curiosity was not yet necessarily anti-religious. Yet, it gave birth to science and philosophy which, after all, are the two names for the self-same thing. The natural religion of primitive people is free from any metaphysical conception. It does not explain the world with the assumption of a single first principle or even as the work of a single creator. The cosmogonies of the Eastern as well as Greek mythology are full of ideas which are no more spiritualist than materialist; they are rather materialist than spiritualist. Through the process of clarification and development those primitive ideas regarding the cause of natural phenomena led first towards materialism, and only later towards metaphysics.

The necessities of life impel man to observe the phenomena of nature. A certain crude notion of laws governing the phenomena inevitably results from the observation. Man looks up at the sky at first neither to worship the all-powerful god in heaven, nor to admire the workmanship of the creator. More profane feelings actuate him to raise his eyes to the sky; it is to watch the clouds in the expectation of rain; to observe the movement of the sun and moon, and to ascertain the location of stars so as to guide his steps in the desert or to navigate his vessels on the water; to anticipate the direction of the wind which might lead his sails to a friendly shore. Similarly, fire is discovered by man not as a god to worship, but as a thing of purely material origin which can be helpful to his physical existence. The primitive man makes his first acquaintance with Mother Earth not as a goddess to be adored, but as an aggregate of clods which, subjected to his labour, bear him food. The struggle for existence brings man face to face with the diverse phenomena of nature, first, in their reality. This relation of man, himself a product of nature, with the phenomena of nature, would awaken in him the striving to discover their cause as well as the laws governing them, were he not tied to the fantasies and superstitions born of the primitive emotion of fear.

Natural religion—the cult of ascribing the diverse phenomena of nature to a variety of gods—brings in its train the class of priests. The gods must be propitiated with offerings and sacrifice, so that the natural phenomena they respectively control may go on normally for the benefit of man. The priests are supposed to be conversant with the mysterious ways of the arbitrary gods, so as to make the offerings and sacrifices acceptable to them. Though made nominally to the gods, the offerings and sacrifices actually become the source of income for the priests. They, therefore, build up an elaborate edifice of rituals and ceremonies on the basis of the primitive nursery-tales. As the intermediary between the helpless man and the powerful gods, the priest acquires a dominating position in society, and shapes its ideology. Under priestly monopoly, the spiritual progress of society cannot transcend the superstitions of natural religion. Eventually, the anthropomorphic gods might be subordinated to a supreme being—also an anthropomorphic conception. Or a sort of precarious monotheism might develop on the decayed foundation of a licentious polytheism. The more likely development, however, is towards pantheism; the other alternative is that of an intellectual curiosity provoking metaphysical speculations which end in the absurdity of declaring the world to be a delusion.

Philosophy, that is, enquiry into the causes of natural phenomena, is not possible under the conditions of priestly domination. Practically in all the lands of ancient civilisation—Egypt, Assyria, India, Persia, Rome—the sacerdotal monopoly of spiritual life prevented the quest for natural knowledge. Human mind is liberated from the superstitions of natural religion, thanks to the rise of a new class of people. Abstract thought originates with a class of people, freed from the drudgery of physical labour, but guaranteed an existence of leisure and comfort by the product of the labour of others. The new class rises as a challenge to the social monopoly of the priest. Its contributions to the development of abstract thought takes the form of philosophy only when it is completely differentiated from the priesthood. The differentiation is the result of the opening of new channels for the accumulation of wealth in the hands of a non-producing class. The non-sacerdotal intellectual aristocracy is usually composed of landlords engaged in the trade with articles manufactured by slave-labour. The necessity of the peasant as well as of the sea-faring trader to observe and understand the phenomena of nature creates in such an intellectual aristocracy, deriving benefit from both the forms of social activity, the impulse for the knowledge of things as they are. Its economic position raises the new class above the childishness of natural religion. An advantageous position in society stimulates its spiritual life. But its economic interest comes in clash with that of the priesthood. In primitive society, the bulk of the surplus product of social labour, that is, whatever is produced over and above the barest necessities of the producers, accumulates in the possession of the priestly class in the form of offerings and sacrifices.

In order to destroy that economic monopoly, the new intellectual aristocracy attacks the spiritual domination of the priesthood. The power of the priest is undermined by the liberation of natural phenomena from the control of their presiding deities. The physical explanation of nature begins. In the absence of any clear notion of a supreme being, or First Principle, the enquiry after the origin and laws of natural phenomena cannot stray into the wilderness of lofty but futile speculation. Philosophy is born, not as metaphysics, but as physical science, to culminate, after a long and chequered career, as the Science or Sciences.

Of all the countries of antique civilisation, Greece alone developed the social conditions suitable for the birth of philosophy. In the rest of them, society remained under the spiritual leadership of the priests. Some failed to survive that state of spiritual infancy; others, sooner or later, came out of the prolonged twilight only to plunge headlong into the darkness of metaphysical speculations which dazzled deceptively as the high-road to absolute truth.

Even in Greece, the honour of being the birthplace of philosophy was reserved for the Ionian and Doric maritime colonies. The famous cities of Asia Minor and Magna Graeçia (Sicily, Southern Italy and North Africa) were economically prosperous and culturally refined. They were great centres of political and mercantile activities which took their intelligent citizens on long journeys overseas and brought them in contact with foreign peoples and strange conditions. The result was the growth of an aristocracy, not only possessed of wealth and political power, but also of a free and enlightened conception of the world. In the seventh century B.C., the Ionian cities were the homes of the knowledge of mathematics, astronomy, physics and engineering. In the following century, Pythagoras transplanted the taste for mathematical and physical studies to the Doric cities. All the illustrious fathers of philosophy—Thales, Anaximander, Heraclitos, Anaxagoras, Democritos, Protagoras, Empedocles—were more or less materialistic in their speculations regarding the origin of things. "Every philosopher, even the most ideal, might be prosecuted as a denier of the gods; for, no one of them pictured the gods to himself as the priestly tradition prescribed."*

Materialism thus was not a perversion of the innate spirituality of man. It was a natural development of the spirit of man, freed from primitive ignorance, and unencumbered by the artificial impediments of the doctrines and dogmas of metaphysics. Ignorance and prejudice persecuted philosophy from its very birth, and eventually succeeded in ovrewhelming it. But modern science has ultimately dislodged the metaphysical usurper from the throne of philosophy, and has restored materialism to that position of dignity.

Not only had Socrates to drink the cup of poison for his impiety, but many other sages of ancient Greece were also prosecuted on the same charge. The free and liberal Athens drove the greatest of her sons, Aristotle, to the protection of Macedonian

* F. A. Lange, "The History of Materialism".

barbarism. Protagoras had to flee, and his books against the gods were burnt. Anaxagoras was arrested, but managed to escape the fatal consequence. Diogenes of Apollonia was persecuted as a denier of the gods. Even in the freer atmosphere of the Ionian cities, Thales, Democritos and others were accused of atheism, because they freed the vision of man from the mist of wonder, and transferred the study of the world from the dazzling fable-land of religion and poetic ideas to the sphere of reason and physical theories. Knowledge has, in course of time, dissipated the ignorance which persecuted philosophy, and those materialist and religious sages of antiquity are vindicated as the truly spiritual guides of humanity.

In India also, dissatisfaction with the Vedic natural religion gave rise to the speculation about the origin of things. Those speculations are recorded rather enigmatically in the Upanishads. But in India, the speculation about the origin of nature did not start from the repudiation of the prejudices of the primitive natural religion, because it was done mostly by the Brahmans, whose very existence as the leaders of society was dependent upon the maintainance of the rituals and ceremonies of natural religion. Therefore, the evolution of thought in ancient India took the latter course of a headlong plunge into metaphysical speculation. Evidences of dissatisfaction with the Vedic natural religion can be traced in a sufficiently early period,—when the Upanishads were composed. They contain fragmentary records of that primitive spirit of enquiry into the origin of things. But the enquiry was not the result of the rise of a non-priestly class which was opulent and therefore intellectually advanced enough for the purpose. It was mostly confined to the priestly class itself, although some Kshattriyas appear also to have participated in it. In any case, little record of the non-priestly contribution to that early enquiry has come down to us. Whatever tended towards the origin of a true philosophy, that is, to the discovery of the causes of natural phenomena in nature itself, must have been suppressed by the Brahmins who retained the spiritual monopoly for a long time to come. In the hand of the Brahmins, the primitive inquisitiveness did not prove disruptive for old traditions. It did not undermine the position of the priesthood. On the contrary, it constructed a speculative system which stabilised the decayed structure of the Vedic natural religion. Instead of challenging the authority of the Vedic gods, and consequently of their ministers, the all-powerful Brahmins, the orthodox Hindu speculation of the Upanishads sought to establish its doctrines, and refute other, more philosophical, systems on the authority of the Vedas themselves. Therefore, the metaphysical speculations of the Upanishads could not even lead to clear monotheism. It could set up only a very precarious form of monotheism. The conception of Brahman was precarious, because it did not necessarily do away with the pantheon of the anthropomorphic natural gods.

The Brahman of the Upanishads is a purely *a priori* assumption—an unverifiable hypothesis. That assumption regarding the origin of things categorically puts an end to all enquiry in that direction; therefore, it renders positive knowledge impossible; philosophy is out of the court, and priestly monopoly of ideology is perpetuated. The basic defect of ancient Indian philosophy was that the origin of nature was not sought in the nature itself. The *a priori* assumption of a super-natural factor inevitably blocked the way to empiricism—the gate to positive science and true philosophy. Later on, there appeared bolder thinkers, such as Kanada, Kapila, Gautama, Charvaka, and others who came more or less near to a mechanistic conception of nature. But even most of them could not completely liberate themselves from the prejudice of some sort of an unknown force giving the first impulse from outside. Owing to that basic weakness, ancient Indian materialism was eventually overcome by metaphysics, and philosophy degenerated into dogmatic theology.

There developed the elaborate form of logic which so successfully fettered human spirit to the prejudice of the ideal of releasing individual souls from the bondage of the physical existence. Brahmanical domination, completely re-established after the Epic Era, checked the "heretical", that is to say, philosophical tendencies of the primitive enquiry recorded in the Upanishads.

The challenge to priestly supremacy had come from the warrior caste. There had not risen any other class able to bid for the spiritual leadership of society. The annihilation of all the powerful Kshattriya clans on the fateful field of Kurukshettra concluded that early struggle of classes in favour of the Brahmins. Consequently, Vedic natural religion was re-established. Yudhistira performed *Asvamedha* not so much to celebrate the victory of the Pandavas as to acknowledge the triumph of the Brahmins, whose monopoly over the surplus product of society was re-asserted through the pompous re-establishment of the Vedic sacrifices.

The death-bed injunction of Bhishma, the doyen of the destroyed Kshattriya clans, clearly indicates the changed relation of classes. He gave victorious Yudhistira the following significant advice regarding the position and treatment of the Brahmins: "A king, to be virtuous, must give the Brahmin offerings. Such offerings are more meritorious than *Asvamedha.* The Kshattriya goes to the heaven as recompense of this virtue. Land should be given to the Brahmins and gods. It is unpardonable sin to take land away from the Brahmins. Don't punish a Brahmin even by mistake, for he is superior to all men. Fire is born of water, Kshattriya of Brahmin, and iron of stone. When iron cuts stone, fire dries water, and Kshattriya becomes the enemy of Brahmin, then, they all lose their force and are destroyed. It is the duty of the king to punish those who claim equality with the Brahmins."

The exhaustion of Indian antique society in consequence of the internecine wars described in the Mahabharata, prevented for a long time the rise of new social forces which might contest the spiritual monopoly of the Brahmins. Subsequent speculations regarding the origin of things all bore more or less indelibly the stamp of Brahmanic prejudices. Even the Vaisheshik and Sankhya systems, the positive outcomes of Hindu speculation, were not entirely free from them. There were more revolutionary thinkers; but owing to the weakness of the social forces constituting their background, their philosophic boldness could not successfully challenge priestly supremacy, and therefore failed to wield an abiding influence over Indian thought.

The priestly domination of society, rendering real philosophy impossible, continued right up to the rise of Buddhism which represented the first open, and temporarily triumphant, revolt against Brahmanic priestcraft and its reactionary effects on Indian society. A glimpse of the picture (drawn by the hand of a non-critical eulogist) of Indian society at the time of the rise of Buddhism, reveals the cause of the "spiritual", that is to say, unphilosophical, character of the main currents of Indian thought.

"Not only had the Brahmans become an organised intellectual which asserted for itself the leading position in political affairs hitherto held by the Kshattriyas, but in ministering to the religious needs of the Indo-Aryan community, they had established a monopoly which lent itself to unscrupulous exactions and to the encouragement of the grossest superstitions. The ancient Vedic idea of the divine power of speech had developed into the philosophical concept of the *Mantram.* A Mantram could bring victory or defeat in wars, assure the prosperity of a State; it could be used to silence the argument of the opponent; it could stop a cough or promote the growth of hair. There was no concern of daily life, great or small, which could not be affected by it. The Brahmanical theory of the Mantram, that it contained in itself a divine principle and the compelling power of the Deity Itself, though its use by ignorant or ill-disposed persons would be ineffectual or disastrous to himself. The influence exercised by unscrupulous or ignorant priests was bound to encourage superstition among the masses, and to become a hindrance to civilisation as well as a source of exaction and cruelty. Another instrument of tyranny and deception, placed in the hands of the Brahmans, was the Aryan belief in the divine power of sacrifice which had come down from the earliest Vedic time. In course of many centuries, the performance of sacrificial rites had grown into a fine art which Brahman experts were not slow to use for their personal advantage, for the efficacy of the sacrifice was said to depend largely upon the liberality of the indispensable *dakshina* or reward bestowed upon the officiating priest. Like the Mantram, the application of Vedic sacrificial rituals extended to every concern of private and public life. The purity of the divine power of the Brahman was said to be implicit in the fact that sacrificial rites were performed for his benefit. And not only did public sacrifices and the worship of tribal deities involve a vast expenditure of State revenue, but the household rites, for which the services of Brahmans were generally necessary, grew more and more numerous and complicated. There were endless sacrificial ceremonies which required the attendance of Brahman experts."*

The Hindu philosophy is, strictly speaking, theology. With the exception of the Vaisheshik and

* Havell, "History of Aryan Rule in India".

Sankhya, no other speculative system tried to explain the origin, evolution and phenomena of nature independent of an assumed super-natural agency. With such an assumption, speculative thought becomes theology—a fruitless enquiry or dogmatic assertion about the nature of the super-natural spiritual being which, by its very nature, is beyond all enquiry and description. However, Hindu philosophy offers the most classical example of the contradictions and confusion of metaphysical thought. The Gita is considered to be the most representative and authoritative work, containing the quintessence of Hindu philosophy. It contains the following remarkable passages: "There is no difference between the material and immaterial. The formless, invisible, and uncreated, immaterial becomes materialised in the same way as water is crystallised into ice."

"Though false as the gleam of a polished shell, or as a mirage caused by the sun's rays, yet no one at any time, past, present and future, can rid himself of the delusion" (of the world).

The most obvious contradiction is the admission of the reality of that which is declared in the same breath to be a delusion. A thing that existed in the past, exists in the present, and will exist in the future, is eternal. The eternity of the "delusion" of the world thus granted, the Brahman necessarily ceased to be what it is assumed to be, namely, "only one without a second". The very foundation of Hindu philosophy is thus blown up.

If the immaterial is really immaterial, the material can never grow out of it. Two things having nothing in common cannot stand in the relation of cause and effect. If the material comes out of the immaterial, then, the latter cannot be what it is supposed to be. It must also be material. Thus, there is but one substance in existence. The dualism is only a sophistry, a verbal contrivance to defend a useless hypothesis. Should immateriality be conceded to the origin of things, then, its very existence would be denied. For, existence, which means, extension in space, is not compatible with the conception of immateriality. Water exists materially; therefore, it can change itself into ice, another material existence. The material phenomenon of ice could never happen, unless water existed as a material substance. Therefore, the material is the only reality, and it exists eternally. That admission is the logical inference to be drawn from the above passages. But such an admission would be highly damaging for the entire system of the Hindu metaphysical thought. It would cut across the vicious circle of metaphysics. It does not leave any room for a creator. The conception of an eternal existence dispenses even with the more elusive hypothesis of the First Principle. Therefore, the start is made from the other end, which eludes verification.

The hypothetical absolute Supreme Being, possessed of flagrantly contradictory attributes, which violate its supposed absoluteness, is assumed to be the only reality; and the undeniable reality of the material world is declared to be a "delusion"! Further, "there is no difference between the material and the immaterial." Yet, according to Hindu philosophy, true wisdom consists of the ability to distinguish between the material and the immaterial. Endless confusion, naturally, results from such arbitrary splitting of the unity of being.

The sum and substance of metaphysical speculation, particularly of the wildest Indian type, can be stated as follows, to make its absurdity evident: Proposition—the finite is not the infinite; problem—how can the finite know the infinite? Solution—the finite must become the infinite!

The Vedanta Sutras, as interpreted by Sankaracharya, represent the acme of the orthodox Hindu philosophy. Yet, the Sutras themselves have actually been differently interpreted. The "*Sri Bhashya*" of Ramanuja, for example, differs from the Sankar-Bhashya on a number of basic points of doctrine. The latter, an admirable work of scholastic argumentativeness and speculative extravagance, is full of self-contradictions. For instance, Sankaracharya admits: "If (there) is a second entity, co-existing with Brahman from eternity, it follows that Brahman has a second." He saw the fallacy of this inextricable dualism which invalidates the basic theorem, "when Brahman is known, everything is known"; therefore, he tries to explain it by declaring the parallel existence identical with Brahman. But that hardly improves the situation. Sankar is generally believed to have expounded a system of monotheism almost as perfect as Hegel's Absolute Idealism. A study of the Sankar-Bhashya, however, shows that the belief is baseless. The work begins with the following passage: "It is a matter not requiring any proof that the object and the subject, whose respective spheres are the notions of the "Thou" (non-ego) and the "Ego", and which are opposed to each other as much as darkness and the light are, cannot be identical."

No less than two major fallacies are involved in this point of departure: Firstly, the basic principle of the system is simply taken for granted, it is not proved; and secondly, an absolutely dualist conception is made the premise of a monist philosophy. Consequently, Sankar had to invent the absurdity of the *Mayavad* (which cannot be traced in the Sutras themselves) to establish the purely spiritual unity of being.

The doctrine of Maya is expounded as follows: "Brahman is associated with a certain power called Maya or *Avidya*, to which the appearance of this entire world is due. This power cannot be called 'being', for being is only Brahman. Nor can it be called 'non-being' in the strict sense, for it at any rate produces the appearance of this world. It is in fact a principle of illusion: the undeniable cause, owing to which there seems to exist a material world. Maya thus constitutes the *Upadhana*, the material cause of the world. Maya belongs to Brahman as a Sakti. We may say that the material cause of the world is Brahman in so far as it is associated with Maya. This doctrine obviously contradicts the conception of Brahman as the unitary and absolute existence. Brahman is devoid of all qualities. Yet, Maya is assumed to be its Sakti. Moreover, Maya is conceived as an existence parallel to Brahman. The idea of "association" presupposes two entities: similarly, does the idea of "belonging".

The most remarkable part of the Vedantic monism is the logic with which the unity and simplicity of Brahman is established. The object of the Vedanta Sutras was to systematise the Aupanishadic speculations into a homogeneous whole, and to prove that the quasi-materialistic (heretical) doctrines of Kanada, Kapila, Gautama and others, were not borne out by those speculations. The Upanishads contain speculations which cannot be reconciled in one system. For example, in the Tchandogya, Brihadaranyak and Taittiriyaka, ether or space (akasa), fire and air are visualised as existences without origin. This view cuts across the basic dogma also set forth in all the Upanishads, that in the beginning there existed the Brahman, "only one without a second", and this dogma constitutes the premise of the cardinal doctrine of Hindu philosophy, namely, "when the Brahman is known, everything is known", also propounded in the Upanishads. In the face of this flagrant contradiction, the entire body of the Aupanishadic speculation would not logically be the basis of a system of philosophy. Unorthodox thinkers daring to challenge the authority of the Scriptures, pointed out this contradiction. They argued: If none but Brahman exists in the beginning, then, ether, air, fire etc. have an origin; that is to say, they are created, and the hypothesis of a creation renders the absolute conception of Brahman untenable. On the other hand, if the elements are without origin, then, the Brahman ceases to be what it is assumed to be—"only one without a second". If one of the views is correct, then, the other is not. Thus, the infallibility of the Scriptures is shaken. Their claim to absolute authority can no longer be maintained. The monism of Vedanta, as interpreted by Sankaracharya, is reared just on this contradiction. In order to obviate any disturbance of the absoluteness of the Brahman, the elements must be without an origin. The difficulty (of dualism or pluralism) is overcome by declaring them to be identical with Brahman.

Sankar's commentary on this Sutra is highly interesting. It gives a graphic picture of the Hindu philosophy, and outlines its curious logic. "These promissory statements (regarding the unity and exclusiveness of Brahman) are not abandoned, that is, not stultified, only if the entire aggregate of things is non-different from Brahman, the object of knowledge; for, if there were any difference, the affirmation that by the knowledge of one thing everything is known, would be contradicted thereby. Non-difference again of the two is possible only if the whole aggregate of things originates from the one Brahman. And we understand from the words of the Veda that that affirmation can be established only through the theory of the non-difference of the material cause and its effect.'...If the ether etc. were not effects of the Brahman, it could not be known by Brahman being known, and that would involve an abandonment of a (previous) affirmation; an alternative which, as invalidating the authoritativeness of the Vedas, is of course altogether unacceptable." The logic is remarkable. If the Vedas contradict themselves, that should not be allowed; since that would affect their authoritativeness! The incontestable authority of the Scriptures is the absolute standard. Should the evidence agaist the infallibility of the Scriptures be found in the Scriptures themselves, that should not be admitted, because that would shake the authority of the Scriptures. The basic principle of this remarkable logic is to submit everything to the test of an unverifiable hypothesis, and to reject all evidence against the hypothesis, simply because they expose its absurdity and renders it untenable. Throughout the ages, Indian speculation has been vitiated by this stultifying system of logic. It was the ideology of a stagnant social order under priestly domination.

To have found the unity in diversity, is claimed as the greatest merit of Hindu philosophy. But, as a matter of fact, the unity was not found. It was simply assumed or imagined. It is an ideal conception which brushes aside the problems to be solved. Since the rise of the material world out of the assumed immaterial root-cause is not logically possible, dualism persists defying all metaphysical verbal jugglery. From the Aupanishadic *Rishis* down to Sankaracharya, no orthodox Hindu speculative thinker was able to prove how the diversities of nature could rise from a common cause. The sheer impossibility of the task ultimately drove Indian speculation to the monumental absurdity of the *Mayavad*. Vitiated by the baffling, but obstinate problem of dualism, the speculation about the origin of the world must necessarily come back again and again to the good old conception of an anthropomorphic god, whose venerable appearance casts a sinister shadow on the sublime light of philosophy. Sankaracharya's laboriously constructed *Advaitavad* solved the problem of the world by the simple contrivance of declaring it to be a dream. Nevertheless, it could not get rid of a personal god. And a personal god is utterly incompatible with the philosophical conception of unity in diversity.

The antique Greek philosophy also could not remain strictly materialistic. Human ideology is determined by the conditions of society, under which it develops. The influence of technology on ideological progress is decisive. The pre-Platonic Greece attained a level of social evolution where human ideology transcends the arbitrary bounds of natural religion. Speculations about the physical origin of things liberated human spirit from the domination of the gods. But experimental science was as yet practically unknown.

The institution of slavery prevented the development of technology. Aristocratic contempt for manual labour isolated theory from practice. Scientific theories are applied to practice, so necessary for the development of tèchnology, only when it becomes necessary to increase the productivity of human labour. But so long as human beings are not differentiated from the beasts of burden, the necessity is not felt. Their labour costs so little that it is more economical to maintain a large number of slaves than to improve the technical means of production. Besides, valuable machines cannot be entrusted to the slaves who are too ignorant to use them fruitfully and, by virtue of their very social position, lack all sense of responsibility. For all these reasons, the bold conjectures of the Ionian physicists could not be verified. The magnificent mechanical conception of the Universe was still to remain a fascinating hypothesis.

Circumscribed by social conditions, ancient philosophy could develop thus far and no farther. That, however, does not minimise the importance of the progress made; and its influence on future development could not be any the less. Even in its inevitable metaphysical deviations, Greek philosophy did not altogether leave the solid ground of materialism. The metaphysical deviation was inevitable in the conditions of the time. Freed from the childish faith of natural religion, thinking minds were eagerly searching for an explanation of things, for a common origin of the diverse appearances. Owing to the difficulties of verification, the conjectures and hypotheses about a purely materialist origin of things could not be generally convincing.

Then, there intervened a new factor which decisively influenced the direction of thought. The growing disbelief in the gods of natural religion had destroyed the old standards of morality. New standards of social and political relations must be found. The conception of a First Principle and Absolute Truth thus became a social necessity. Goodness and badness, equity or otherwise, of terrestrial things—political institutions and social relations should be judged not on their own merit, but in comparison with an imaginary perfection. The problem of social relations diverted the mind of man from the speculations about the cause of the natural phenomena; ethical problems overshadowed physical enquiry.

Pythagoras and Anaxagoras represent the transition of Greek philosophy from primitive materialism to metaphysics and ethics. The position of the latter, who eventually became the source of inspiration of eighteenth century rationalism, is highly interesting. Anaxagoras remained enough of a materialist to teach that knowledge could be derived only through the senses; but at the same time, he declared sense knowledge to be delusive. He reconciled this contradiction with the doctrine that reason was the regulating faculty of the mind which was nothing but the sum total of sense-perceptions. Thus a new divinity was invented to dictate the conscience and conduct of man. But what is this mysterious entity Reason? How can its judgment be infallible? Reason itself is nothing but an abstraction of knowledge previously acquired through sense-perception. Not being able to analyse reason (which could be done only with the aid of the advanced knowledge of physiology), Anaxagoras left the firm ground of materialism, and drifted on the shifty sands of idealism. The doctrine of reason, as an independent agency, obliged him to take another step still farther away from his original position. He postulated a Universal Intelligence to explain the infallibility of reason.

The doubt about the reliability of knowledge, acquired through the senses, had been much more rationally and effectively dispelled by the old materialist Heraclitos who declared that "senses fail only the barbarian soul; rightly educated senses gave true knowledge." But the conditions for the right education of senses were not yet there. Owing to the backwardness of technology, exact knowledge of things could not be had as yet.

The setting up of some abstract standard of truth, however, was not an empty metaphysical declaration. It was the ideological reflex of the striving for the creation of a centralised State. The aristocracy, striving for supreme power over the democratic communities, needed an authority for their pretension. An absolute principle governing the Universe supplied a very plausible authority for a centralised, all-powerful State on earth. The nature is so harmonious, because it is governed by the principle of absolute wisdom, truth and perfection. To be harmonious and happy, human society should also be guided by wisdom and truth. But there are but a few wise, truthful and perfect men in this world. The government of society, therefore, should be entrusted to those few hands. The State could not exist without a wise ruler, just as a ship could not do without an experienced pilot.

With this anti-democratic philosophy, Athens became the centre of the political as well as the cultural world of the Greeks. But the Sceptics and Sophists vented democratic resistance of this philosophy of political absolutism. Both the schools drew inspiration from the teachings of the earlier materialist philosophers. By deposing the gods from their thrones, the physical conception of the origin of things had promoted scepticism as regards religion. The haziness of the quasi-materialist speculations which resulted from the then impossibility of demonstrating the correctness of the mechanistic hypothesis, contributed to the spread of scepticism to the entire realm of enquiry for knowledge.

The founder of the sceptical Eleatic school,

Xenophanes, on the one hand ridiculed the poetical polytheism of Homer, and attacked, on the other, the growing custom of keeping knowledge confined to a small circle of the elite. Following fruitlessly the speculative path in the search for a satisfactory knowledge of things, he came to the conclusion that nothing can be known for certainty. The pretension of those, who claim to know the way to perfect wisdom and absolute truth, was thus challenged. Scepticism was the ideology of the democratic middle-class which desired to overthrow the domination of the priesthood, on the one hand, and to combat, on the other, the growing supremacy of the aristocracy. But it was a purely negative factor. It pulled down the moral authority of all the established institutions, but was not able to replace it with a new standard. It was the ideology of the impending dissolution of the antique society. It could not be successfully combated by the moral philosophy of Socrates. A new religion—revealed monotheism—was the effective antidote to the disease. Plato's idealism heralded the rise of the new religion.

Ever since the fall of ancient materialism, neither speculative philosophy nor religion nor theology was able to explain the old question about the why and how of things. The first half of the question itself is absurd, and any attempt to answer it will be necessarily also absurd. The other part of the question is pertinent, and materialism alone can give a satisfactory answer to it. The answer given by speculative philosophy, religion and theology, is that things are so simply because they are made so by an arbitrary creator or an inscrutable First Cause.

The logical conclusion of this "philosophy" is that man, as a mortal with limited capacities, can never know anything; he is doomed to eternal ignorance so that the nature may always remain an impenetrable mystery to veil a hypothesis which cannot stand the test of knowledge. Man's only consolation is to contemplate an enigma that will always be beyond his comprehension.

Scepticism was a protest against this monstrous madness raised, in the interest of the ruling class, to the dignity of wisdom. But the well-warranted protest of the Sceptics was futile, since the weapon which alone could cut the Gordian knot, though roughly cast, was still to be perfected. It was with the potent weapon of materialism, so ingeniously sketched by the philosophers of ancient Greece, that European spiritual life eventually took up the effective struggle against the monstrous sentence of eternal ignorance.

Scepticism encouraged a healthy critical attitude, and disregard for absolute authorities. The Sophist philosophy was the immediate positive outcome of antique materialism. Instead of declaring, like the Sceptics, the attainment of knowledge to be an impossibility, the Sophists recognised the reality of knowledge. The founder of Sophism, Protagoras, was a pupil of the materialist Democritos. He held that the cause of all phenomena was in the common substratum of matter. From this materialistic general proposition, he inferred that everything is true relatively. Men have different perceptions at different times, according to the changes in the objects perceived. Therefore, every sensation is a true sensation. That was a refutation of the dogma of eternal truth and absolute knowledge.

Speculative philosophy was driven to a tight corner. The philosophical triumph of Sophism would mean a social revolution. According to the Sophists, nothing was wrong or right by nature; there were no fixed standards. So, neither the current codes of law and morality, nor the established political institutions could be immune from subversion. They were all conventions, set up by the necessity of circumstances, and therefore must disappear with the change of circumstances, to give place to new codes of law and morality and new political institutions. That revolutionary, dynamic view of things was very dangerous to the established order of society. The Athenian aristocracy combatted the revolution with a gigantic philosophical reaction, associated with the venerable names of Socrates and Plato.

Until the great social crisis, revealed by the spread of Sophism, philosophy had been apparently detached from the questions of daily life. It was occupied in the search for a solution of the grand problem of the Cosmos. Notwithstanding its speculative deviations, it was based upon a rudimentary, largely hypothetical, and often mistaken, scientific study—of astronomy, mathematics, physics and mechanics. Socrates made ethics the only concern of philosophy, and his pupil Plato completely pushed aside the scientific enquiry of earlier thinkers in favour of metaphysical speculation.

Social stability, the supremacy of the ruling class, was conditional upon fixed ideological standards. The Sceptic doctrine of the uncertainty of all knowledge and the Sophist view of the relativity of truth, destroyed all old standards. Socrates rather demagogically than boldly met the Sceptics on their own ground, and inferred from their doctrine that "the gods did not wish men to penetrate their secrets." He argued that therefore man should seek certainty where he could find it,—in his own consciousness. He advised men to be concerned with themselves, and leave things divine (that is, the problems of the Universe) to the gods. For proposing this unphilosophical, but none the less irreligious, division of labour between man and god, the Athenian sage had to put on the crown of martyrdom. But only in that primitive rationalism could he find a weapon to fight the more powerful disrupters of the established order, namely, the Sophists. They denied any external fixed criterion of truth. Socrates retorted that it was in man himself, an integral part of his being. He held that all men could be just, because justice resided in their consciousness; they could be good and wise, because goodness and wisdom were similarly innate in themselves. Subjective and, therefore necessarily variable, conceptions of justice, wisdom, goodness, virtue etc. were thus raised to the status of objective realities, fixed standards of truth.

Having postulated that the eternal truth, the fixed standard of knowledge, resided in the consciousness of man, Socrates set about to explain how the light could shine so as to show everybody the right way of life. Men's minds were full of "incoherent and unscientific notions," that is, variable ideological standards growing out of changing objective conditions. Socrates taught that those notions should be cleared away, and "scientific notions", that is, absolute criteria, should take their place. Then, the divine light in man would shine brilliantly. He argued that all men agreed that wickedness should be punished. But confusion would be inevitable unless there was a generally accepted idea of wickedness. Therefore, true knowledge was conditional upon correct definition of terms, and definition was the statement of the objective characters of general terms. That method was applied to all the questions raised by the Sophists, namely, what is justice? What is virtue? What is morality? What is law? so on and so forth.

Thus began the search for an absolute objective reality in subjective conceptions which, by their very nature, are necessarily changeable. The conscience of man should be the standard for the correctness of definitions. Apparently, this basic dogma of the moral philosophy of Socrates comes very near to the fundamental maxim of Sophism: "Man is the measure of all things." But in reality, there is a world of difference. The "man" of the Sophist is not an abstract conception, but a concrete phenomenon, always changeable under varying circumstances; with Socrates, conscience is an absolute standard. According to him, justice, goodness, virtue etc., are not variable abstractions from concrete individual phenomena, considered, under a given set of conditions, to be just, good, virtuous, etc. They are absolute categories, innate in man's consciousness, independent of all changes of the circumstances in which the man lives. All acts of man that might measure up to these arbitrarily fixed absolute notions, as it were sucked out of the thumb, should be considered just, good, wise, virtuous etc.

A completely new chapter in the history of philosophy was opened. Introspective speculation replaced physical and cosmological conjectures. Ethics and metaphysics gained precedence over science and enquiry into the origin of things. Owing to the admitted failure to reach any certainty, knowledge had come to be discredited. Wisdom became the noble ideal of man; and anything enigmatical came to be known as wise.

The memorable reaction in the intellectual development of mankind (though inevitable in the objective conditions of the epoch, it was nevertheless a reaction) is depicted as follows by a philosophical historian: "Socrates turned the subject matter of discussion from physics to ethics. General and abstract terms and their meaning stood out as the capital problems of philosophical research, and the governing agents of the mind during the process; in Plato and Aristotle, we find the meaning or concept corresponding to these terms, invested with an objective character, and represented as a cause or beginning, by which or out of which real concrete things were produced. Logical, metaphysical, ethical entities, whose existence consists in being named and reasoned about, are presented to us as the real antecedents and producers of the sensible Kosmos and its contents, or as eternal with the Kosmos, but as its underlying constituents—the primordia or ultima—into which it was the purpose of the philosopher to reduce sensible things."*

Previously, philosophy had endeavoured to explain nature as satisfactorily as possible under the conditions of the epoch. Socrates deprecated such speculations as futile. In his hand, philosophy herself changed her native character and turned her face to the opposite direction. Socrates held that science could not be taught; that is, knowledge was not to be acquired empirically. It could only be drawn out of one's own self.† Man should search not for the knowledge of things, but for intuitive wisdom—in his own being. Man should abandon the ambition of knowing, and glorify the fantasies of his ignorance as intuitive wisdom—the infallible guide in a world never to be known. From an infinitesimal particle in the grand cosmic mechanism, man became a being, raised above nature whose laws were to submit themselves to his impertinent ego. The noble liberatrix of human spirit was thus prostituted by the petty egocentrism of the pedantic moralist. Philosophy was so wantonly violated, because the material interest of the ruling class was antagonistic to the spiritual liberation of the race.

But moral philosophy cannot stand by itself. In order to be an unfailing guide for the conduct of man, his conscience should cease to be the property

* Grote, "History of Greece".

† The similarity with the Hindu doctrine of "Atmadarshan" is unmistakable. Such evidence proves the utter groundlessness of the complacent assertion that Hindu philosophy begins where the Western ends. The unphilosophical point of departure is not a monopoly of Hindu philosophy.

of a terrestrial being, and take on the character of a spark of a self-illuminated and all-illuminating celestial light. In other words, an arbitrarily set up earthly standard could not claim infallibility except with the sanction of an absolute principle, force or being, which knows no law. Plato provided the moral philosophy of Socrates with this prop. He affirmed the possibility of attaining absolute truth through "the confidence in the truth of universal propositions", that is, absolute ideas. In support of this new dogma, he made the following metaphysical, non-verifiable, assertions:

> "Propositions are equivalent to the natures they affirm; therefore, those (propositions) which relate only to Essences (of things) and Ideas are indisputable (truths); those which relate to the world of senses, dealing only with copies of Ideas, are less and less trustworthy in proportion to their sensuous nature; they are, at best, only probabilities, whereas universal propositions are primary truths, seen to be such by intuition."

Philosophy was thus shifted from the ground of enquiry into the nature and origin of things to the realm of mere mental gymnastics. The examination of objectively existing things was abandoned for the contemplation of subjectively conceived ideas which were dogmatically endowed with objective reality, and things were declared to be mere shadows. The source of all knowledge was "conversation with one's own soul", and true knowledge could be derived only from such esoteric communion, because individual souls were parts of the omniscient Universal Soul.

Not only was the foundation of Idealism laid, but the way was open for the return of religion on the ruins of which philosophy had risen originally. The anthropomorphic gods of the decayed natural religion were replaced by more ethereal entities, Absolute Ideas, to tyrannise human spirit all the more effectively. Plato is the real father of Christian theology, and Platonic metaphysics, together with Christian theology, throttled philosophy for nearly two thousand years, until the birth of modern science provided materialism with the necessary weapon in the struggle for the spiritual liberation of man.

Even the very father of Metaphysics, Aristotle, stood with one foot on the solid ground of materialism. A disciple of Plato, he nevertheless rejected the poetical extravagances of the Master, and endeavoured to place speculative philosophy on a plausible foundation of reality. He preferred the analysis of the world as it existed to the flight in empty abstractions. He held that the general law could be discovered only through the examination of particular facts. Plato had declared that knowledge acquired through senses was deceptive. Aristotle discarded that view which cut at the root of philosophy, and maintained that without sensation there could be no thought; that the knowledge of particulars could be gained only through the senses; and that from the knowledge of particulars, by induction, the knowledge of the Universe is attained. Aristotle criticised the Platonian speculators with the following materialistic arguments:

"Their thoughts are not directed towards the

phenomena and the discovery of their causes. They endeavour to make the phenomena correspond with their opinion. Treating of the phenomena, these philosophers say things which by no means correspond with the phenomena; the cause of this is that they have not rightly conceived first principles, but reduced everything to certain preconceived notions, and they persist in this (false philosophy) in spite of all contradictions, as if they were in possession of true principles, as if these ought not rather to be deduced from the phenomena."

Aristotle shatters the very foundation of idealism by denying the objective existence of ideas. He holds that ideas exist only subjectively, being the product of reason which abstracts the general law from the particular phenomena perceived by senses. He traced not only the inanimate nature to a material origin, but even visualised a spontaneous generation of the vital phenomena out of the same material substance. He was of the opinion that living beings—animals and plants—grew out of matter through "its own original force". To substantiate this view, he pointed out for example the breeding of moths from rotten wood, of flees from decomposed dung, of lice from damp wool etc.

Thus, the father of metaphysics himself avoided the unphilosophical dualism of mind and matter, which eveneually became the foundation of metaphysics. Aristotle understood that there could be no philosophy except on the basis of the recognition of the reality of natural phenomena. But in the conditions of his time, he also could not put his empiricism into practice. In the absence of the technological means for "educating the senses", so that they could acquire exact knowledge of particulars, the balance inclined on the side of the Universals which were conceived as the categories of pure logic. In the beginning, so very clearly coloured with materialism, the system of Aristotle, however, is vitiated by the confusion regarding the function of Logic. With him, logic was not merely an instrument of thought; it was also an instrument for the examination of external things. He understood that true knowledge could be acquired only through the perception of things as they exist; yet, he tried to gain the perception rather through contemplation than from an actual examination of the concrete. In the absence of material possibilities, to acquire exact knowledge of things, and of their relations, empirically, hastily formed ideas pushed the objects to a secondary place, and ideas assumed the character of independently existing objects of investigation. And logic becomes the instrument. In this form, philosophy inevitably degenerates into formalism and wild speculations.

From the proposition that all knowledge is based on some previous knowledge, Aristotle concluded that universal conception is the standard of truth. Crassly contradicting his own empiricism, he laid down: "Sensations are less trustworthy than ideas." So, the Platonic dream of an objectively existing absolute idea was smuggled in through the backdoor as the pivot of Aristotle's metaphysics. Beginning empirically, Aristotle's system degenerates into speculation: His physics becomes metaphysics. This transformation takes place so unreasonably that even a sympathetic critic is bewildered by the somersault of the "Universal Mind" and remarks: "He seems so cautious and judicious when indicating the first steps, that we are surprised to find him suddenly on the other side, with no bridge visible over which he could have passed."*

Bridge or no bridge, Aristotle did cross the Rubicon. He had not rejected Plato's "Absolute Idea". He simply did not think that such a thing, as it were hanging in the air, could be the dependable basis of a metaphysical system which was to combat and replace old materialism; which could convince the Sceptics and silence the Sophists; in short, which could provide the ideological foundation for the feudal-catholic social order to rise on the ruins of the antiquity.

An arbitrary standard of human ideology—an arbitrary cosmological conception—was necessary to prepare the ground for an arbitrary power on earth. Socratic ethics was too pedantic to be practical. Platonic idealism was too obtuse to carry general conviction. Trained in the sound school of materialism, the Greek mind was too scientific and rational to be so easily stampeded. Antique democracy was a thing of the past; but its traditions still swayed the popular mind. Under those conditions, an abrupt break with materialism would only discredit philosophy. The system of Aristotle represents the transition. Empiricism and speculation, physics and metaphysics, are placed side by side—to be fitted into a casual chain. But being mutually exclusive, they can never stand in the relation of

* Lewes, "History of Philosophy".

cause and effect. Hence, Aristotle's system must reach a point of abrupt break with materialism.

The break takes place where Aristotle abandons empirical enquiry for logical contemplation. He maintains that "the general principles are known by themselves, whereas knowledge of particulars, through which the general principles are reached, is only known to us." With this fallacious argument, he establishes the dogma of "the germ of knowledge with which the soul is born"—a dogma which has been the stumbling block of philosophy throughout ages, up to Kant. It was finally destroyed by modern biological discoveries. The theory of evolution has proved conclusively that innate ideas or instincts or intuitions or the "*a priori* elements of human knowledge" are also results of experience previously gained through the senses. Aristotle himself visualised this possibility, but was driven into the vicious circle of metaphysical speculations under the pressure of social and historical forces which always determine the character of philosophy.

Ancient philosophy had visualised the Universe as in an eternal process of change. Neither materially nor spiritually can mankind keep standing at one place, abide by eternal principles—except that of change. A perspective of continuous progress was opened before humanity by ancient philosophy. But there must be a fixed standard of truth so that the ruling class might be armed with a moral authority to combat, on the one hand, the tendencies of social dissolution, and to curb, on the other, the pretensions of a revolutionary democracy.

Aristotle established the standard with the aid

of formal logic, which replaced the ancient dialectics and for centuries cramped human mind into artificially conceived categorical notions. Formal logic gave birth to the pernicious doctrine—"It is impossible for the same thing to be and not to be"—on which the elaborate structure of metaphysics and theology was raised to overshadow throughout the middle-ages the fire of human knowledge kindled in the antiquity. By this logic, all the basic dogmas metaphysics and theology are set up negatively, because they cannot be proved positively.* If a thing, rather a conception or notion, is proved not to be this or that, then, it must be admitted to be something else. The hypothesis of Absolute Idea or First Principle or God is "proved" by this logic. But this is no longer philosophy. It has been correctly observed that mediaeval thought is only theology and logic, but there is no trace of philosophy in it.†

Scepticism, promoted by the dissolution of the antique society, drove speculative philosophy to seek the shelter of faith,—this time not in the gods of natural religion, but in the new dogma of Revelation. The positive outcome of Aristotle's metaphysics was to lay the philosophical foundation of Christian monotheism.

---

* The Hindu doctrine of "Neti Neti" is a notorious application of the method of negative proof. You start from a preconceived notion (of Brahman) which is endowed with super-natural attributes. Then, you compare things perceived by the senses with the imaginary, unverifiable, entity. Since none of the really existing things can measure up with the imaginary ideal, this is "proved" to be something above, beyond and independent of, the phenomenal world. The entire mediaeval European thought was vitiated by this pernicious "spiritualist" mode of thought.

† Prantel, "History of Logic".

Individualism, in the sense of the emancipation of man from the tutelage of imaginary gods as well as from the tribal patriarchal sacerdotal social relations, was the philosophy of Greece in the days of her glory. The striving for the freedom of the individual reached the high-water mark in Sophism. Socrates, Plato and Aristotle unsuccessfully combatted the Sophists. The rise of moral philosophy and its necessary evolution into Platonic idealism and Aristotelian metaphysics were the spiritual reflex of a socio-political reaction—the attack of the "Tyrants" and the Spartan aristocracy upon the Athenian democracy. Poisoned to the core by the institution of slavery, antique society was however doomed to dissolution. Neither a democratic nor an aristocratic nor again a despotic State could save it from the inevitable fate. Although Sophist individualism philosophically implied abolition of slavery, the Athenian democracy was not in a position to do so in practice. It did not represent a higher form of social labour. Consequently, the struggle which eventually caused the downfall of the antique society, was only for the control of the State based upon the social relation of slavery. Such a State could be stable only on the foundation of an authority which laid down laws, itself being beyond laws.

Plato and Aristotle constructed the ideology of such an absolute State, but the ideal could be realised not in Greece, but on the ruins of the Hellenic freedom. The great founders of speculative philosophy which dominated the civilised world for nearly two thousand years, were the heralds, politically, of the Roman Empire, spiritually, of the Christian

Church, and socially, of feudalism. European humanity eventually began the struggle to break the chains forged by Platonic idealism and Aristotelian metaphysics only when the materialist and individualist philosophy, combated by those sages of Greece, re-asserted itself.

Sophist individualism succumbed not so much before the attack of Platonic reaction, as under its own contradiction, growing out of the social conditions of the time. Indeed, Sophism was the bridge over which ancient philosophy passed from materialism to metaphysics.

Protagoras was the first to replace the object—external nature—by the subject—man—as the starting point of philosophy. His position was analogous to that of the eighteenth century sensationalism (Locke, Condillac etc.) which was the common starting point both of modern idealism and materialism. Protagoras stood in the same relation to Plato as Locke later on to Berkeley. As soon as sense-perceptions are declared to be the *only* sources of knowledge given to man, the certainty regarding the nature of the external object can no longer be asserted, because there is no certainty that our perceptions are true representatives of the external things; and this uncertainty inevitably leads to the denial of the objective existence of external nature. The Sophists stood on this slippery ground. Their enthusiasm to emancipate the individual from all bondage lured them away from the safe base of strict materialism. For Democritos, the atom was the "thing in itself". His disciple Protagoras, however, regarded matter as something undetermined because it was in a process of continuous change. He was eager to free the individual from all bondage, even of the materialist determinism. But the rejection of, or disregard of, the law of casuality inherent in nature, logically leads one to the quick-sand of metaphysics; nay, indeed, to the morass of Faith. If the natural phenomena are not determined by the laws inherent in nature itself, then, they must be produced and governed by some supernatural force, or even by anthromorphic gods.

Thus, by its own implications, Sophism played into the hands of its opponents. Socrates himself began as a Sophist, and opened his attack upon Sophism with the weapon forged by its own contradictions. The social background of slavery drove the Athenian democracy into such an ideological vicious circle. The revolutionary significance of Sophist individualism was vitiated by the exclusion of the producing multitude from democratic freedom. The slavery of the multitude, on whose labour society subsisted, required an ideological justification, and that would naturally be incompatible with a constructive individualism. The bondage of slavery, tacitly retained, impelled Sophist individualism to deviate either towards idealism or Scepticism. The sensationalism of the Sophists, by implication at any rate, justified slavery, and therefore could not possibly be the ideology of a new social order. The indeterminism of Protagoras meant that things have no significance except in their mutual relations. Applied to social relations of his day, this apparently materialistic principle turned out to be a justification of slavery. The institution of slavery was of no consequence. It was good or bad, beneficial or harmful, according to its relation with other classes of society. If it was bad and harmful under an aristocratic or despotic State, it could be good and beneficial when the State would be democratic. The denial of casual relation in nature was parallel to the disregard for the fact that the social phenomenon of slavery also had a cause, and therefore could not be different under a democratic State, so long as that cause remained in operation. Indeterminism in philosophy, moreover, was a result of the inability to detect the casual relation between social and political phenomena and, conversely, led to the failure to understand that slavery as the means of production must necessarily produce a specific type of State which could never be really democratic.

One of the cardinal principles of materialism also is that sense-perception is the foundation of all knowledge. The implication of this principle is the denial of innate ideas. Consciousness does not exist independently of outside things. But when it is asserted, as was done by Sophism, and more clearly by modern sensationalism, that we have only our *own perceptions* of things, the firm ground of materialism is abandoned. For, the starting point of materialism is the acceptance of the objective reality of things. The relation between the perception of a thing and the thing itself has been for ages the bone of contention of speculative philosophy. The development of natural sciences has put an end to that idle disputation. None claiming any scientific knowledge would to-day doubt that our conception of a tree corresponds with the tree itself. Any such doubt has been dispelled since man began to get acquainted with nature through his activities. When a thing reproduced by man, according to his perceptions, corresponds with the original object of his perception, there can no longer be any possible doubt about the objective reality of things and the correctness of our perception of them. The foolish dispute persisted so long as man tried to know nature only through passive contemplation. Once the taste of the pudding has been ascertained by the simple but convincing method of eating it, there can no longer be any doubt about it.

The doctrine that we have only our own perception of things must lead either to idealism or Scepticism. In order to establish its basic principle of the relativity of knowledge, as opposed to the dogma of Absolute Truth, namely, "man is the measure of all things", Sophism exaggerated the value of sensation at the cost of the objective world. The subjective factor of consciousness overshadowed the objective existence of things, so that the latter were to recede in the realm of doubt, or even forfeit their reality. Sensationalism rendered Sophism only a prelude to the Platonic doctrine of Universals and to Aristotle's "Formalism". Things do not exist independent of thought; they are the incorporation of Ideas as Plato held; and Aristotle put the same doctrine in a different way: Forms precede matter, the latter becoming concrete particular by fitting itself into the corresponding form. There are not only abstract ideas of goodness, justice etc., but also, for example, of "horseness", "treeness", "stoneness" so on and so forth. The unknown and undetermnied matter becomes the concrete phenomena of a horse, tree, etc., by incorporating the ideas of "horseness", "treeness", etc.

Thus, thanks to its unconscious idealistic deviation, Sophism prepared the ground for metaphysics. Its negation was born in its own womb. Originally a Sophist, Socrates ushered in the philosophical reaction against Sophist individualism. Athenian democracy was defeated; with it also ended Greek freedom. Unable to face squarely the cardinal social problem of slavery, Sophist individualism lost its revolutionary implication and degenerated into the ideology of social dissolution. The new philosophy justified slavery as a "natural" thing, and thus became the ideology of social reconstruction; but that precarious process could take place only at the expense of political freedom. The fathers of "spiritualism" were not content only with providing the ideology of political reaction. They actively participated in the destruction of Greek democracy and liberty. Leading disciples of the saintly Socrates secretly aided the Spartan aristocracy in the struggle against Athenian democracy. The godly Plato sought favour in the courts of "Tyrants" —those destroyers of antique freedom. Aristocratic Sparta was the ideal of his "Republic". Aristotle placed himself at the services of the Macedonian Philip, who subjugated Greece to a foreign rule.

While preparing the ground for the Roman State and the Christian Church, the ideological reaction, immediately, stimulated Scepticism which was also inherent in the Sophist philosophy. Traditional Greek rationalism, with its roots struck down in a materialist and mechanistic conception of the Universe, could not be easily satisfied with the poetry of Platonic Idealism or with the formality of Aristotle's Logic. If the immediately given perception of senses did not supply them with correct pictures of external things, how could the knowledge of anything be ever possible? Social disintegration placed the stamp of boundless individualism and pessimism upon philosophy. Indeed, philosophy itself appeared to be irreparably discredited. In order to save itself from the disgraceful end, philosophy again came down from the ethereal regions—and sought for a footing in the world of realities. Materialism re-asserted itself.

Three currents of thought flowed out of the social crisis. The first, represented by the Alexandrian school, appeared to abandon philosophy and concentrated itself on the cultivation of experimental sciences; but in doing so, it rendered the most valuable service to the eventual resurrection of philosophy. The other two currents were represented by the Stoics and the Epicureans. Both those schools rejected the metaphysical speculation of Plato and Aristotle, and sought inspiration in the older materialist tradition. The Stoics started from the quasi mystic Heraclitan cosmological conception, because it provided a plausible basis for their politico-moral doctrine, having for its object the curbing of individualism in the benefit of the general. The altruistic moral and Republican politics of the Stoics were adopted by the early Christians. Their materialistic determinism consequently degenerated into teleology. Nevertheless, the Stoic philosophy was essentially pantheistic, which destroys the dualist conception of the Universe, and therefore is distinguished from materialism only by a very thin and often imperceptible line. Later on, with Spinoza and Hegel, the greatest of modern philosophers, Idealism drowned itself in the ocean of pantheism which, in its turn, merged into scientific materialism.

The metaphysical speculations of Plato provided Christianity with a philosophical foundation, not only plausible, but veritably profound. The sage of Athens completely abandoned the rationalist methods of ancient Greek thought, and plunged headlong into a contemplation of the First Cause of things, which was supposed to exist without being material. The consequence was that Platonic Idealism postulated a hierarchy of the First Cause, Self-Generating Will and the Universal Soul, which subsequently became the triple pillars of Christian theology.

The doctrine of the spiritual superiority of the Indian culture is based upon an ignorance of the history of Europe from the downfall of Greece to the close of the dark middle-ages. European thought during that long period of fifteen hundred years was intensely "spiritual". It was strikingly akin, in all essentials, to what is fondly believed by the Hindus to be their proud privilege,—a special genius of their race. But the historical fact is that, for several centuries after the establishment of the biblical faith as the State religion of the Roman Empire, the intellectual life of the entire Christian world was engrossed in the highly obtuse speculation about the nature of the Supreme Being, and in the futile attempt to solve the baffling problem of the creation of the material world out of nothing by an incorporal and impersonal agency. Gibbons' famous account of the evolution of Christian theology is prefaced by the following observation: "The latter (Trinitarian controversy) was a high and mysterious argument, derived from the abuse of philosophy. From the age of Constantine to that of Clovis and Theodoric, the temporal interests of the Romans and barbarians were deeply ivnolved in the theological disputes of Arianism."*

Of all the schools of Greek thought, Stoicism bears the most striking resemblance to Hindu philosophy; and Stoicism was the prelude to the rise of Christianity. The austere morality and lofty idealism of the Stoics went directly into the making of the faith of the early Christians. Christianity drew its inspiration also from neo-Pythagorean mysticism —that quasi oriental mystic cult introduced in the Roman world on the fraudulent authority of the old philosopher. Resting upon such a rich background of speculative thought, emotional exuberance and mystic cults, the naive monotheism of the Bible was rationalised by the gigantic intellect of Aristotle. The elaborate system of Christian theology was buttressed stoutly upon Aristotelian logic, and became the authority for the highly learned scholastic rationalism which dominated European thought for many hundred years.

No religion is born in a day—revealed to a particular prophet. The doctrines and dogmas of each religion crystallise themselves in a process,

* "Decline and Fall of the Roman Empire".

over a whole period of history. It is a period of social transformation. The change in the conditions of material life brings about a corresponding readjustment of ideal standards, although these are considered to be precedent to, and independent of, the mundane world. The disruption of old social relations shakes the basis of a particular form of faith. Man's relation to god or gods, as the case may be, is determined by the relations among men themselves. Natural religion, as for example of the Vedas, or of the Greek mythology, is the deification of the diverse phenomena of nature as objects of worship. It is the religion of the decentralised tribal society. Monotheism, the belief in one God, rises as the ideology of a centralised State. The worship of a glittering galaxy of gods, all equally powerful idealised human beings, is the spiritual expression of man living in the state of primitive democracy. The idea of one God or a Super-God, becomes a social necessity as a spiritual sanction for the monarchic State rising on the ruins of tribal freedom. An over-lord in Heaven is postulated as the sanction for an over-lord on earth.

The development of the religion of a particular group of human beings from polytheism to monotheism is influenced by the intensity of the social crisis under which it takes place, and of the maturity of the forces of further progress. Either there is a complete break with the past, and monotheistic faith gains ground as the mighty lever to revolutionise social relations; or the conception of a sort of Super-God grows out of the background of polytheism, as a compromise between the old and the new. The latter development represents a continuation of the social crisis, the urge for progress being too weak and halting to clear away the decayed old.

The spiritual progress of India followed the latter course. Vedantic monotheism—that of the Upanishads—did not replace the older form of faith. Instead, it rationalised primitive polytheism. The reason for such an involved process is to be found in the relation of social classes which constituted its background. The new monotheistic doctrine was not sponsored by a new class with a spiritual outlook free from tradition. It did not appear as a standard-bearer of revolt against the established rites and rituals which fortified the dominating social position of the priestly class. The dissatisfaction with the old faith was voiced mostly by individual members of the priestly class, and remained confined to them. Naturally, their dissatisfaction could not and did not go to the extent of advocating complete abolition of a form of popular form and worship which had placed their class at the head of society. The monotheism preached by them was not a new popular faith. It was a mystic cult which largely remained a monopoly of the priesthood, and consequently reinforced their social position. The new cult did not condemn the old faith, on the contrary, recommended it as the religion suitable for the vulgar. An airy structure of mystic monotheism was thus reared upon the foundation of decayed natural religion. The new faith was not the result of a striving to free the individual from the bondage of the tribal society. It fortified the position of the anthropomorphic gods by placing them in a Pantheon, the inner mysteries of which were accessible only to the Brahmans. The Hindu brand of monotheism, strictly speaking, is pantheism. It is the ideology of an unsolved social crisis,—of social stagnation.

The absence of a strictly monotheistic cult in religion reflected the political disunity of India. The social forces favouring the establishment of a centralised State, having failed to attain a sufficiently high level of development, the growth of a strictly monotheistic faith was an impossibility. The first centralised State in the history of ancient India was the Empire of Asoka, and that happened under the revolutionary banner of Buddhism. That also disintegrated, revealing the lack of an abiding social cohesion. The subsequent Empires of Chandragupta and Harshavardhan were more transient political phenomena. The outstanding feature of the political history of ancient and mediaeval India is the absence of a centralised State. The obvious reason of that characteristic feature was the inadequacy of economic conditions, and weakness of the social forces associated therewith. The occasional subjugation of the entire country, or of a considerable part thereof, in great Empires, was not an organic growth; it was an artificial creation as was testified by their quick disintegration. Even those Empires were not centralised States. Their structure was that of a loose federation. So long as the country remained broken up into more or less self-contained village communities, forming here and there isolated economic regions, a centralised State was an impossibility. The condition of political union would be the disruption of self-contained local economy which could happen only in consequence of the rise of new modes of production. That condition developed very slowly, owing to the insufficient margin of social balance—itself a result of the primitive mode of production necessarily associated with self-contained village economy. Hence, India never experienced political unity and did not develop a strictly monotheistic religion.

Christian monotheism triumphed as the ideology of a whole period of human progress, because it rose out of a background of complete racial dissolution, advocating the establishment of new social relations to be governed by revealed spiritual standards.

The rise of a new trading class in the countries around the Levant had disrupted the tribal social organisation, ideologically as well as economically. Previously, land had been held in common, and cultivated by collective labour for the maintenance of the entire community. The appearance of trade altered the character of agriculture. Its function ceased exclusively to be the feeding of the community. Its product, in larger and larger quantity, came to be exchanged, yielding profit to those engaged in the new occupation, namely, the traders. With the object of bringing the product of agriculture completely under their control, the traders acquired the possession of land. The creation of private property in land destroyed the communistic organisation of society. Private ownership inevitably led to the concentration of land in big estates. Tribal chiefs and heads of clans became landlords or kings. Those, who had previously cultivated the land as free members of the community, were transformed either into tenants or slaves, toiling for the landlord, producing no longer food for the community, but commodities for exchange in distant markets. The disruption of primitive communism, the evolution of private property and the growth of trade contributed to the rise of cities, populated by classes of people entirely divorced from the land either by choice or under obligation. The cities were centres of trade as well as of manufacture by slave-labour. The merchant-princes therefore lived there by choice. The number of artisans, performing labour in the bondage of slavery, was swelled by the influx of toilers driven away from the country-side by the decomposition of the common ownership of land. Trade destroyed the economic self-containedness of the communistic rural social units. Goods manufactured in cities by slave-labour penetrated there in exchange of agricultural products, and destroyed village handicraft. Finding themselves superfluous in the village, owing to the subversion of the communistic structure of its economy, rural craftsmen also drifted to the cities. There, they swelled the ranks of slaves, or enjoyed the dubious freedom of the pauperised "citizens" living upon the munificence of the merchant-princes who had ruined and transformed them into social parasites.

The economic dislocation of society and its structural redistribution brought about a parallel process of confusion and recasting of ideology. The idea of a life after death was absent in the primitive communistic society. Man had no individual existence apart from, and outside or independent of, the tribal organisation with which he completely identified himself. While alive, he was an integral part of the community; after death, his individual being was merged in the collective existence. He continued living in the life of the community. The institution of ancestor worship evolved in that state of primitive culture. Assured that even after death the community would take care of him, the member of the primitive communistic society was not bothered by the problem of the life after death. As a matter of fact, death appeared to him very much like a prolonged state of sleep. In that state of primitive bliss, the speculative thought of man was concerned with the external nature with which he was in constant struggle, and whose diverse phenomena were wonders for him. He was impressed by the regularity of natural phenomena, he also found them to be benevolent or stern or cruel. Yet, far from the state of metaphysical absurdity, he could not conceive of things acting without a cause. By nature, man is not "spiritual", but rational. Extensive observation of the primitive peoples still living in various parts of the world, and critical study of history, have conclusively established that the idea of soul, god or some mystic essence of nature evolves at a comparatively late stage of civilisation. In the beginning, man assumes that there must be a tangible cause for each natural phenomenon. Since his thought is limited by his own being, he imagines the phenomena of nature as actions of corporal beings like himself; only he visualises those beings immensely more powerful because of the immensity of their deeds. The recognition of superiority carries with it the feeling of admiration or fear. Just as superiors on this earth can be adored by devotion or placated by offerings, just so was the attitude towards the unseen celestial beings. Thus men created gods after their own image.

The first form of religion proper (magic and fetishism precede it in the process of ideological evolution) marked as much the beginning of faith as of science. It is not the result of any "spiritual" urge in man. It is not the evidence of his innate faith in forces super-natural. It does not prove that even the primitive man has a higher self which transcends the limitations of his corporeal existence, and seeks satisfaction in communion with the divine essence of things. It proves that the spiritual life of man consists of his eagerness to know the world in which he lives; and this eagerness is a purely biological function. The highest product of nature, the human organism, is equipped with the capacity of acquiring unlimited knowledge of things which surround it, inciting it constantly to activities of diverse kind,—sensual, nervous, cerebral and creative. With the appearance of human organism, adaptation to natural environments ceases to be the motive force of evolution. The struggle for human existence is the struggle for the domination of the forces of nature; and knowledge of the diverse phenomena of nature is the condition for human existence and progress.

The inquisitiveness of man, which leads to the establishment of natural religion, is also the first impetus to the birth of science. Natural religion is built upon the sound principle of causality,—nothing happens without a cause. Even magic, the ideology of the savage, is based upon a hazy notion of this sound principle. Science also starts from this principle. Therefore, as long as man remains in close touch with nature—throughout the period of primitive communism—religion is but the naive form of nascent science. Science begins with the question regarding the cause of things. As soon as the regularity of the diverse phenomena of nature is detected, and the casual connection underlying them is even vaguely surmised, natural science is born. The superstitions of polytheism are not decisive checks upon reason. This is a human faculty more primitive than faith, which rules out reason as incompatible with the "spiritual essence" of man. Full of absurd superstitions, polytheism, in its primitive purity, nevertheless is not vitiated with metaphysics. Faith, not buttressed upon the imaginary rock of revelation, is bound to be half-hearted, ready to make compromise with reason, if the latter promises greater knowledge of nature than can be acquired by the grace of gods.

The rituals and ceremonies of natural religion are so to say technological contrivances for controlling the forces of nature for human welfare. The primitive man does not strive for the salvation of his soul from the bondage of nature. The absurd notion that he is not a part of nature is not his. He is free from the illusion that his real self is something apart from, and beyond the realities of, life. He lives too close to the Mother, to deny her existence. His concern is with things of this world.

After death, his individual existence would be submerged into that of the community; or he would attain the celestial home of gods, and acquire the power of gods, to control the forces of nature more effectively than by sacrifices, ceremonies and rituals.

The scientific essence of natural religion, however, cannot outgrow its superstitious form until social evolution brings into existence a class of people free from the care of getting the means of subsistence by manual labour, and therefore in a position to contemplate nature with detachment. So long as man lives too close to nature, he is overwhelmed and terrified by its phenomena. No rational thinking is possible under such conditions. Just as a picture can be duly appreciated only from a certain distance, just so can the nature as a whole be visualised in correct perspective only when contemplated from a distance. So long as in his daily life man feels himself to be a helpless victim of the forces of nature, it is not possible for him to take a rational attitude towards them; for, such an attitude presupposes detachment, and there can be no detachment when the relation is that of subordination.

The rise of cities detached a section of the antique society from the close association with nature. The expansion of trade and development of manufacturing industries quickened that process of social differentiation. There rose the class of merchant-princes—landlords engaged in opulent trade—which was in a position to develop the scientific essence of natural religion. By virtue of its freedom from the necessity of earning livelihood by manual labour, which implied helpless subordination to the forces of nature, the new social class was no longer overwhelmed by them. Thus, it was able to look upon the forces of nature not with awful veneration, but to observe them in their casual connections. Nor was such observation a purely intellectual pastime. It was a social necessity, connected directly with the economic being of those engaged in it. The merchant-princes themselves, in their daily life, were no longer at the mercy of the forces of nature. But their power, position and prosperity were based mainly upon the two branches of social activity which were subject to those forces. Agriculture and navigation (for the purpose of trade) required observation of the diverse phenomena of nature. That observation, made by a class of people not subjected in their daily life helplessly by the forces observed, produced results ruinous for the natural religion which had contained the germs of the observation.

The detection of a mechanical regularity of the diverse phenomena of nature undermined the primitive faith in gods. Rain, lightning, thunder, storm, rise and fall of temperature, ebb and tide, movements of the heavenly bodies—all these and many other phenomena closely associated with the daily life of man were not the actions of arbitrary deities. They happened necessarily, as inevitable effects of given causes, governed by laws inherent in nature itself. When close observation of the phenomena of nature, and the calm of contemplation of its result dispensed with the necessity of propitiating imaginary gods by means of rituals and sacrifices, science was born in the form of primitive philosophy which was naturally materialistic. The devotion to gods was replaced by the desire to discover the mechanical laws of nature. The blind faith in super-natural beings yielded place to the inquisitiveness about the origin of things which was sought in nature itself. That inquisitiveness led to the rise of philosophy in the true sense of the term.

# CHAPTER II

## THE ORIGIN OF MATERIALISM

THE Greek thinker Thales has been called the father of philosophy. He is also honoured as the founder of the physical science. He disbelieved the divinity of the agencies causing natural phenomena. He saw that a rational explanation of nature was impossible as long as its phenomena were attributed to imaginary gods. Therefore, he discarded the old notion that all natural events were caused by the arbitrary and inscrutable volition of gods. Having set aside the old superstition, he began the search for the origin of phenomena in nature itself: for a material cause of all things, without any mystery or myth.

Along with all the other great Ionian physicists of his time, Thales did not distinguish between matter and a moving principle. They were all monists, and as such true philosophers. In their time, when science was just in the throes of birth, the knowledge about the origin of things could only be an ideal. But it was one of the greatest achievements of pure thought to have placed that noble ideal before mankind. In the beginning, there could be only plausible conjectures and working hypotheses. The rejection of the dogma that the world was produced and governed by super-natural, inscrutable and unknowable forces, opened an era of free enquiry which was pregnant of unlimited possibilities. Human mind declared its independence of the bogeys of superstition, set up by the ignorance of its own infancy. The potential power to harness the forces of nature for his benefit separates man from his less developed animal ancestors. To be conquered, the nature must be known; conversely, accurate knowledge of nature can be acquired only in the process of conquering it. That is to say, science and philosophy must develop simultaneously, one helping the other. So long as man stands before nature, baffled, overawed, full of superstition, he can neither know nor conquer it. Science and philosophy begin only when man gathers the courage to tear down the veil of mystery from the face of nature, and becomes conscious of his mission to conquer it.

"Independent of philosophy, the nature exists by itself. It is the ground on which man, himself a product of nature, grows. Outside nature and man, there does not exist anything. The higher beings are the creation of our fantasy. They are merely the fantastic reflections of our own being."* The starting point of modern materialism was thus stated in the middle of the nineteenth century. Twenty-five hundred years earlier, practically the same revolutionary declaration had been made by the Ionian physicists.

Searching for a common natural origin of things, Thales took water for the basic element. Anaximander conceded the place to air. The latter, however, maintained that the elements like water, air, fire etc. must be traced to something more ulti-

* Ludwing Feuerbach. "The Outcome of Classical Philosophy".

mate. He regarded the elements as variable, subject to conditions. As a working hypothesis, he assumed a final existence—the "all", which was infinite. The assumption smacks of metaphysics; but his reasoning makes it evident that by "infinite" Anaximander simply conceived the entirety of all elements out of which the common existence of all things originated, as he visualised, "by separation". His disciple Diogenes of Apollonia traced "the reason that regulated the world to the original substance of air". He came to the conclusion that the Universe was a living thing, spontaneously evolving itself, all its transformations being caused by its own vitality which he identified with air. Heraclitos considered fire to be the original substance. He told that "the world was created neither by God nor by man; it was, is and shall ever be, an ever living fire in due measure self-kindled and in due measure self-extinguished.".

Apart from the attempt to give a physical explanation of the Universe, Heraclitos also enunciated the elementary principles of the materialist theory of cognition. He considered the senses to be the sources of true knowledge. But his permanent contribution to materialism was the foundation of dialectic logic, which destroys the absurd conception of absoluteness. "All things are in a perpetual flux. All is and is not, for though, in truth, everything comes into being, yet it forthwith ceases to be." The bulk of the work of Heraclitos is lost. The existing fragments are formulated rather in aphorisms. But the iconoclastic implication of the above formula is unlimited.

The dialectic logic of Heraclitos, elaborated by Hegel twenty-five hundred years later, is the most formidable weapon of modern materialism. By pulling down absolute entities and immutable standards, it undermined theology and metaphysics; by visualising the world as a process, in continuous change, it opened before mankind an unlimited perspective of progress. It abolishes the fiction of absolute truth and perfect knowledge, but frees the mind of man from all arbitrary limitations. Human knowledge is never perfect; perhaps it will never be; but there is no limit to its scope. This remarkable freedom of spirit enabled Heraclitos to declare: "Whatever is common, is true; the exceptional is false. "What is beyond the comprehension of the mortal mind, is not truth, but a dream; not wisdom, but an illusion. This philosophical principle rules out faith with her train of miracles, super-natural powers etc. What is beyond human understanding, is deceptive. There is no truth which is not acceptable to the senses.

The founder of the much maligned school of Sophism, Protagoras, thought the gods to be the result of the insufficiency of knowledge. The basic principle of his philosophy—"man is the measure of all things"—indicated the surest way to the knowledge of things. What is perceived by man really exists, and that which cannot be perceived by man does not exist. Not only is the existence of the inscrutable, supernatural forces doubted, but the dogma of absolute truth and perfect knowledge is also refuted. Protagoras laid down the principle that real knowledge could only be acquired empirically. Human mind should abjure the giddy, but useless flights in the void and stand firmly on the ground of concrete facts.

Even Empedocles, who deviated from the ground of strict materialism towards Platonic metaphysics, thought that all things were the product of a combination of primary elements, which were fire, water, earth and air. "There is nothing but a mingling (of the elements), and separation of the mingled, which are called birth and death by the ignorant. In spite of his metaphysical tendency, Empedocles held the materialist view that ideas were the result of the impressions of objects received through the senses. In his opinion, changes of thought took place according to changes in the organism of man. By holding this view, Empedocles vaguely pointed the way to some of the basic discoveries of modern biology, which have contributed ultimately to the triumph of materialism. His speculations about the growth of organisms in successive stages indicated the way towards the discoveries of Lamarck and Darwin. The ancient Greek scientists thought that nature tried all possible combinations until there resulted a creature with life, capable of propagation. The affinity with the modern biological theory of adaptation is evident. The Universe is not conjured out of nothing by the miraculous hand of a creator, nor is it the permanent miracle of something growing out of nothing. It is the result of a purely mechanical process of continuous adaptations—of endless production and annihilation—in which finally that alone survives which bears in itself the guarantee for persistence and progress.

Ancient materialism became a comprehensive

system in the hand of Democritos. Several hundred years later, it was further developed by Epicuros. The atomist theory propounded by the former, and perfected by the latter, ultimately became the foundation of modern science. The atomism of Democritos contains the skeleton of the materialist philosophy. The following are its main propositions:

1. Out of nothing arises nothing; nothing that is, can be destroyed. 2. All change is only combination and separation of atoms. 3. Nothing happens by chance; everything has a cause and happens of necessity. 4. Nothing exists but atoms and empty space. 5. The atoms are infinite in number and of endless variety of form. They are falling eternally through the infinite space. In course of the fall, the greater impinges on the smaller. The collision produces lateral movements and vortices. Thus commences the formation of worlds. Innumerable worlds are formed and perish successively and simultaneously. 6. The atoms have no internal conditions, and act on each other only by pressure and collision. 7. The soul consists of the finest and most mobile atoms which permeat the whole body, and produce the phenomena of life.

These propositions contain many notions which, in comparison to our present scientific knowledge, may appear crude, childish and even ludicrous. But the merit of ideas, evolved two thousand five hundred years ago, should not be judged by the standard of to-day. What is to be admired in these propositions is that they contain the germ of modern science: That the early materialist conception of the

Universe, though overwhelmed by religion, theology and metaphysics, which dominated human thought for nearly two thousand years, survived all the vicissitudes of history, to become the weapon in the struggle for the spiritual liberation of man.

The first proposition contains the two basic principles of modern physical science, namely, the indestructibility of matter and the conservation of energy; the second lays down the corner-stone of a strictly mechanistic cosmology. These principles make no room for a creation of the Universe. Together, they keep the human mind away from the fantastic doctrine of creation out of nothing—a doctrine which strikes at the very root of all philosophy. Out of the two first propositions, the third logically follows. It is a decisive negation of teleology. In it lie in embryo, the scientific theories established so many centuries later by Descartes, Newton, Boyle, Kant, Laplace and many others. All the phenomena of nature are governed by the mechanistic laws followed by the atoms in their eternal motion. The materialistic denial of Final Cause is misunderstood or misinterpreted by the advocates of teleology or predestination as a belief in a blind chance. The third proposition of Democritos leaves absolutely no room for such misunderstanding. It clearly rules out chance, and visualises necessity as the lever of every happening. Materialism does not admit accident or chance any more than it tolerates the teleological doctrine of Final Cause or the religious dogma of predestination.

A happening is called accidental when its cause is not yet known. Philosophy does not admit ignorance as testimony to the existence of inscrutable super-natural forces. Confronted with a phenomenon, as yet unexplained, it simply pleads temporary ignorance, and sets about to know the unknown. Otherwise, all physical investigation and exact science would be impossible. The beginning of the quest for positive knowledge could be made only with a plausible hypothesis. Democritos supplied it. Discoveries made in course of subsequent investigations, made possible by the hypothesis, verified it, corrected its mistakes, removed its defects, and have finally established it as a scientific theory. The discovery of the mechanistic laws of nature has cleared away the prejudice of a Final Cause, and has theoretically established the view that nothing happens by chance: Every happening is necessary, has its cause.

The fourth proposition offers the basis for a rational explanation of nature. The foundation of all great discoveries of physical science has been the reduction of the phenomena of nature into the motion of the smallest particles of matter. The atomic theory has led to the discovery of the laws of sound, light, heat and all other physical and chemical changes.

The fifth proposition sketches a picture of the rise of the Universe from the mass of smallest particles of matter in constant motion. In the light of modern scientific knowledge, this picture may appear rather childish. It was not only a vague conjecture, but contained mistaken notions. Nevertheless, the picture as a whole represented a bold penetration into the mysteries of nature. Once the nature was reduced to a conglomeration of the smallest conceivable particles, a hypothesis regarding the combination and separation of atoms becomes necessary for a rational explanation of the Universe. The atoms must somehow come together so that bigger bodies might be formed. The diversity of the size of the atoms is the weakest point in the system of Democritos. It means that the common denominator of all phenomena is not reached at the atoms; for, the diversity of their size proves that the stage of indivisibility has not been reached. The bigger atoms, at any rate, can be split into parts equal to the smallest.

These are the logical flaws of the conception of Democritos. But any criticism of the antique atomic theory from the point of view of modern physical knowledge would be out of place. Democritos had to contrive some way out of the difficult problem of *action at a distance*—a problem which baffled not only Newton, but the entire physical science still for a long time. Unless the atoms were of equal size, they would fall in endless parallel lines, and nothing would ever come out of their motion. Another flaw in the grand conception of Democritos was the vagueness of the notion of space. If space was conceived as an absolute void, diversity of size would not make any difference in the speed of falling bodies. Aristotle seized upon this flaw and made it the pivot of his attack upon the mechanistic conception of the Universe.

With all his vagueness and defective notions, Democritos carried out his speculations strictly according to physical principles, and for the first time gave a complete rational explanation of the Universe. Scientifically, his views have been greatly corrected and amplified; philosophically, however, they remain as valuable as ever. Had Democritos, or even all the Greek materialists taken together, said everything there is to be said on the question, then, they could not be what they were. For, materialist philosophy visualises an endless progress of knowledge. It was not possible to know all at once, what has since been known in course of twenty-five centuries. To claim perfect knowledge, one must believe in divine revelation. Physical enquiries, undertaken on the basis of the conjectures and hypotheses of the Greek materialists, progressively increased the store of human knowledge which, in its turn, corrected the mistakes of the original conjectures, and verified the hypotheses into theories.

In the sixth proposition, the baffling problem of action at a distance is dealt with. The root of metaphysics can be traced to this problem. The failure of ancient materialism to offer a convincing solution to this problem caused the deviation of philosophy to metaphysical speculations. Time and again, metaphysics maintained its shaken position by making capital out of the inability of earlier materialism to explain the phenomena of sensation. The problem could not be solved experimentally in that epoch, owing to the backwardness of natural science. The anxiety to get round the problem lured ancient materialism to corrupt itself with metaphysical deviation. By his effort to rid the system of Democritos of the weakness on the question of action at a distance, the last Greek materialist, Epicuros, compromised with metaphysics. Democritos himself, however, was categorical on the point. The absence of experimental science did not permit him to be so, scientifically. But philosophically, he left no room for ambiguity inasmuch as he denied the atoms any internal conditions, that is, sensation. The materialistic unity of the origin of things is strictly maintained in the atomism of Democritos. The movement of the original substance is purely mechanistic. No hand of the creator shapes it into diverse forms, nor is consciousness an inherent property of matter. The atoms are purely material bodies which move according to purely physical principles, and being in themselves without sensation, produce sensation, that is, thought, as the result of particular forms of their combination. The motion is inseparably associated with the very being of the atoms. By the logic of their very existence, they act upon each other; so, no supra-material internal condition, such as attraction and repulsion, sympathy and antipathy, love and hatred, attachment and detachment, so on and so forth, as postulated by many speculative thinkers, is necessary for them to coalesce and assume successively higher and higher forms. The whole process is mechanistic, taking place necessarily, in an interminable causal chain. The primary movement of fall necessarily causes impingement, and the consequent lateral motion of the atoms; the lateral motion, in its turn, produces collisions which cause vortices. The process becomes more and more complicated, and operates strictly according to mechanistic laws. The Universe grows out of this process, as proved later on, with a mathematical precision, by modern physicists since the time of Kant and Laplace.

In view of this purely materialistic conception of the atom and its movements, it is evident that no metaphysical deviation is to be detected in the seven propositions. Obviously, the term 'soul' is used as a *facon de parler;* for, the souls are also composed of atoms, and atoms are purely material, without any internal condition. The soul-atoms, therefore, must move, like all other atoms, strictly according to mechanistic principles. Their combination produces the so-called vital phenomena. When chemistry was practically unknown, and biology was a thing of a very remote future, the ancient philosopher could not be expected to visualise any more clearly the transition of matter from the *unorgana* to the *organa.* But he did conceive, though rather vaguely, of a process of differentiation of matter into the organic and inorganic without abandoning the ground of strict materialism. In the light of modern biological knowledge, particularly of physiology and psychology, the Democritan conception of soul-atoms and their properties becomes highly interesting. If Democritos was mistaken, it was on the side of exaggeration. He might have confounded consciousness with brain, thought with mind. But few psychologists even of our days can avoid the mistake of confusing the organs with their functions and properties.

The vulgar parody on materialism—"eat, drink and be merry"—is associated with the name of Epicuros, who gave ancient atomism the final shape in which it eventually became the foundation of modern physical science. The moral teachings of Epicuros, and the simplicity of the life lived by himself and his disciples, give lie to the malicious misinterpretation of his philosophy.

In India, Charvak and his philosophy received a similar malicious treatment from the Brahmanic reaction. For maintaining the very sensible view that there is nothing after death, all sorts of absurd and atrocious doctrines were attributed to him, and his authentic teachings were destroyed. Fortunately, Epicureanism escaped such a fate, and came down in history as an impetus to modern science. But only fragments of the very voluminous writings of its exponents have been saved.

The modern world has been correctly acquainted with the philosophy of Epicuros through the famous didactic poem "De Rerum Natura" by Lucratius Carus. The spirit of Epicureanism is beautifully portrayed by the Roman poet. "When human life to view lay foully prostrate upon earth, crushed down under the weight of religion, who showed her head from the quarters of Heaven with hideous aspects, lowering upon mortals, a man of Greece ventured first to lift up his mortal eyes to her face, and first to withstand her to her face. Him neither story of the gods, nor thunderbolts, nor heaven with threatening roar, could quell, but only stirred up the more—the eager courage of his soul filling him with desire to be the first to burst the fast bars of nature's portals."*

Until its true spirit was revived by the resear-

* Translated by Monroe.

ches of the rationalist French clergyman Gassendi in the seventeenth century, the common notion of Epicureanism was based upon the interpretation of the unscrupulous and opportunist Roman lawyer Cicero. The Roman ruling class prostituted the teachings of Epicuros for their purpose. "The theory of Epicuros was in every way purer and nobler than the practice of these Romans; and so now two courses were open to them—they either allowed themselves to be purified and became modest and temperate, or they corrupted the theory, so combined the conception of its friends and foes, that they ended in having a theory of Epicureanism which corresponded to their habits."*

In the last days of the Roman Republic, when Greek learning and culture was fashionable, Stoicism and Epicureanism were the dominating schools of thought. The Romans were as yet too crude to appreciate any of the two contending schools fully in the light of their vast theoretical background. Eminently practical as they were, the Romans rushed to practice Epicureanism without grasping its theoretical foundation. Political greatness and the consequent economic prosperity had corrupted the primitive simplicity and austerity of the Romans. A social crisis, as evidenced by the civil wars, had shaken old virtues. The Epicurean doctrine of happiness was welcome as a philosophic garb for the pleasure-seeking patricians. The essence of Epicureanism is the striving for freedom. With the Romans, devoid of any cultural tradition, and unable to think abstractly, freedom degenerated into

* F. A. Lange, "History of Materialism".

libertinism. The "practical materialism" of the Roman Epicureans offered the Stoics the opportunity to paint Epicureanism in lurid colours—the form in which it was popularly known for ages. Lucratius, therefore, begins his poetic exposition of the Epicurean philosophy with the question: "Does it lead us into the paths of immorality and sin, because it had torn down and trodden under foot the religion which once cruelly oppressed mankind?" The answer, given in the light of the real teachings of Epicuros, is decidedly in the negative.

Epicuros held that happiness was the object of life. The doctrine found an enthusiastic welcome among the patricians of pre-Christian Rome; but later on, it was severely censored by Christianity. Applied to the masses of the people, such a doctrine would be of a highly revolutionary consequence; therefore, in the interest of the ruling class, it must be suppressed. In combating Epicurean materialism, Christian spirituality only served the mundane interest of the ruling class.

The basic principle of Epicureanism is stated in his definition of philosophy: "The activity that makes man happy through knowledge." Epicurean happiness thus is obviously not carnal pleasure. It is spiritual calm, to be attained not in blind faith or idle dream, but in knowledge.

Epicureanism traced its descent directly from ancient materialism, and handed it down to the posterity in the least adulterated form. The positive outcome of the ancient Greek culture was the scientific aciehvements of Alexandria and Epicurean philosophy. They are two links which connect modern civilisation with the ancient, through the fifteen centuries of mediaeval darkness.

Scepticism and its inevitable consequence, pessimism, could be checked either by a relapse into faith or by the discovery of a sure road to knowledge. or by the discovery of a sure road to knowledge. The Stoics led the way in the former direction, whereas Epicuros asserted the possibility of acquiring knowledge of things by reviving the materialist and mechanistic conception of nature as expounded by Democritos. When, as a schoolboy, he was taught that the Universe arose from chaos, Epicuros asked: "And whence came the chaos?" The teacher had no reply to satisfy the inquisitive pupil. Neither was it available from moral philosophy nor from metaphysics. The eager quest for a rational cause of things led Epicuros to the old atomist theory.

National downfall had broken all the old ties of life in Greece. In despair, thinkers were seeking consolation in some form of faith, and thereby falling into all sorts of superstition. Epicuros placed an object before life. It was to find happiness in the knowledge of the cause of the external orders of the Cosmos. Constant changes in society as well as in nature caused great anxiety in human hearts, because people did not know what might happen next. They stood trembling before an unknown fate which appeared to be inexorable. Only the knowledge of the cause of those changes could free man from the tormenting fear either of the unknown after death or of the oblivion of death itself. The knowledge that change is a necessary process, inherent in things themselves, regards it with calm, free of terror, and it raises man above superstition. People believing in the myth of gods are made miserable by the feeling that they are helpless victims of arbitrary celestial beings. Others are unhappy because death will put an end to their existence. But it is just as foolish to feel ourselves helpless victims of imaginary gods, as it is unreasonable to regard the necessary phenomenon of death as an evil. Owing to the very fact that it puts an end to our feelings, we should be quite indifferent to death. As soon as death comes, we exist no more; therefore, there is absolutely no reason to be concerned with what happens after death. A thing is evil when it causes us pain; since death can cause no pain, it is no evil to be afraid of. We cannot feel either pain or pleasure when we do not exist.

Following this line of contemplation, Epicuros arrived at his doctrine of happiness which later on became the object of such malicious misinterpretation. But one can easily realise how different is his conception of happiness from what it was made out to be, when it is known that Epicurean pleasure is not to "eat, drink and be merry", but knowledge. Knowledge of the causes of the constantly changing things frees man from the fear and anxiety which arise from the feeling of helplessness, and that freedom makes man happy. That being the case, to seek happiness is the object of life. Epicuros taught that every pleasure is good, every pain is evil. Every pleasure is good, because it results from knowledge; pain is evil, because it is caused by ignorance.

The confusion about the moral teachings of Epicuros results from two things: His opposition to Stoicism—which eventually became the foundation of Christian ethics; and his bitter attack upon religion. The Stoics held that virtue is happiness, whereas Epicuros taught that to be happy, one should be virtuous. Superficially, there seems to be little difference between the two points of view. Philosophically, and by practical implication, they are, however, like poles apart.

Starting with the common object of finding consolation for the distracted individual, to rescue him from the stormy sea of Scepticism, the Stoics set up the doctrine that the highest realisation of the individual existence is to submerge itself into the general; Epicuros, on the contrary, came to the conclusion that, to be free of all superstition and arbitrary limitations is inherent in the existence of the individual. It was this quintessence of Epicurean philosophy, rescued by Gassendi in the seventeenth century, that became the most powerful weapon in the struggle for the spiritual liberation of the European humanity from the thraldom of the Catholic Church.

In the light of this philosophical difference, a vast diversity is detected beneath the superficial similarity of the Stoic and the Epicurean doctrines of happiness. According to the Stoics, virtue is the thing in itself; it should be practised for its own sake. The practice of this or that virtue may actually cause pain; yet it should be practised because the happiness is not in the result of the practice, but in the practice itself. The result may be unhappy;

nevertheless, one should feel happy simply by practising virtue.* This doctrine divests happiness of a real existence. It can be felt only in imagination. One can never be really happy or unhappy. It all depends on how one feels or rather imagines. The restlessness of the individual is not to be cured by the removal of the cause. It is to be quietened by the application of a drug. Resignation and submissiveness came to be the noblest human virtues. The ideological foundation of the Roman State and Church was laid by the Stoic philosophy.

With the Epicureans, on the contrary, virtue is the means to an end, which is happiness. The two are not identical. A particular virtue is virtue as long as its practice makes one happy. The corollary to this proposition is that, as soon as the practice of a particular virtue ceases to make one happy, it is no longer virtue. Thus, Epicuros not only combated the Stoic doctrine of servility, but liberated human mind from the rigid artificiality of Aristotle's logic. Reverting to the dialectics of the older materialist thinkers, he held that man cannot be happy unless he is wise, noble and just; and, conversely, one cannot be wise, noble and just without being really happy. Wisdom, nobility, justice, are not abstract categories. They are relative, changeable, conceptions, determined by the standard of happiness which, in its turn, is derived from knowledge. Since the knowledge of things reveals them in a process of constant and continuous change, it destroys all fixed standards of virtue.

---

* The analogy with the doctrine of *Nishkam Karma*, expounded in the Gita, is evident.

The individual was restless in the bonds, artificially placed upon his spirit. Epicuros shattered the bonds, and the individual became calm in the contemplation of the endless perspective of knowledge opened up before him. Well in advance of his time, Epicuros went much farther. For him, contemplation was not a tacit attitude. He taught that nature had placed man in such a position that he must act, and knowledge is acquired in the process of the action of man. Reflection and enquiry take place in consequence of the contact of man with external objects; then, ideas develop in an endless process. This theory of cognition struck at the root of Scepticism which had been unsuccessfully combated by all the other systems of ancient philosophy ever since it left the firm ground of materialism. Faith, resurrected by Plato, rationalised by the Stoics, and later on culminating in the new religion of Christianity, only served to hush the tantalising voice of doubt. It was censored, not satisfied. Epicurean materialism offered calm to the spirit, tormented by doubt, by asserting the possibility of endless knowledge.

Since his doctrine of happiness, to be attained through knowledge, could be established only on the basis of a materialist and mechanistic conception of nature, Epicuros necessarily set aside the mythical gods and was hostile to religion. He taught that deliverance from "the degrading and demoralising influence of religion" was the essential aim of philosophy. But he pursued the aim with a remarkably dispassionate calmness. His very atheism and irreligiosity were softened by a flavour of piety. He denied the existence of gods with the singular argument that to believe in them, as beings concerned with material things, was to deprive them of their godliness. If the gods are what they are believed to be—eternal, immortal, super-natural, beings—then, their very nature makes it impossible for them to do what they are supposed to do—cause and govern the phenomena of nature. It is an insult to their heavenliness to believe that they occupy themselves with earthly things. All the events of nature proceed according to natural laws inherent in nature itself, without interference from the gods. This respectful way of bowing the gods down their throne was as ingenious as it was effective. For this, Epicuros naturally incurred the undying hatred of the priesthood. Although its faultless piety and sublime disinterestedness recommended Epicureanism to the early Christians, and its respectful dismissal of the anthropomorphic gods appeared to clear the ground for monotheism, yet, the very godliness of Epicuros was the deadliest attack upon religion. Critical examination of the origin of Christianity has revealed that the idea of endowing a person with divinity might have emanated from the Epicurean prescription: "A noble man should be elected as the representation of God, so that he may look upon us live, and see us act." Traced to such an origin, the doctrine of the divinity of Jesus appears in its mythical nature; consequently, the entire edifice of Christianity, reared upon that doctrine, collapses.

For a philosophical basis of his irreligious morality and godless piety, Epicuros resorted to the atomist theory of Democritos. In the atom, he found a picture of his conception of the individual. Democritos had conceived a mechanistic physical system without any motive. Epicuros adopted it as the foundation of a system of ethics. Therefore, he subjected it to some modifications to suit his purpose. Epicurean modifications of the atomist theory, however, solidified the foundation of materialism, although introducing in it some elements of discord. Aristotle had seized upon the weakness of the theory of the impingement of atoms in fall, to refute the whole Democritean hypothesis. Aristotle's objection was in the line of modern physics,—in a void space, all bodies, irrespective of size, would fall with a uniform speed; hence, there could be no impingement necessary for the atomic motion to become more and more complex.

In order to meet the objection, Epicuros conceived the atoms deviating slightly from the straight lines of their fall. The modification was necessary also to serve the purpose of his philosophy—to endow the individual with a free will, without the intervention of any factor outside nature. While introducing an element not compatible strictly with materialism, the modification nevertheless freed the atomist theory of its obvious defects, putting it in the shape in which it was made the basis of modern physics by Descartes, Newton, Boyle, Heuyghens and others.

The doctrine of the deviation of atoms has been interpreted as a conscious effort on the part of Epicuros to desert the ground of strict materialism. From the fragmentary remains of his voluminous works, it cannot be ascertained what was his motive.

In any case, the doctrine does not necessarily affect the mechanistic nature of the movements of atoms. It does not introduce the element of consciousness in primal matter. On the contrary, it amplifies the crude mechanistic conception of Democritos, so as to obviate the possibility of any dualist degeneration of the atomist hypothesis. However questionable it may appear from the point of view of a strictly materialist philosophy the Epicurean doctrine of atomic deviation does not go contrary to the later development of physics. (Descartes' theory of the vortices, Newton's Law of Gravitation, the nebular hypothesis of Kant and Laplace.) As a matter of fact, these later developments throw an entirely different light on the Epicurean picture of atomic movement. The doctrine of the deviation of falling atoms may be connected with the Newtonian discovery that the heavenly bodies gravitated towards each other. The generalisation of the Law of Gravitation can easily be reconciled with the deviation of atomic motion. The revolving motion of the nebulae can be visualised as the extremely complex development of the Epicurean deviation of atoms.

The Epicurean restatement of the atomic theory leaves no room for any possible dualism. "Out of nothing, nothing comes, for otherwise, anything could come out of anything. Everything that is, is body; the only thing that is not body, is empty space. Atoms are indivisible and absolutely immutable. The atoms are in constant motion. While they approach each other, they combine. But of this, there was never a beginning. The atoms have no qualities, except size, figure and weight."

These basic principles of Epicurean physics clearly visualise the atom being without any intrinsic quality. They have only external motion, from which results the combination of atoms, and the formation of larger bodies. The suspected metaphysical deviation of Epicuros has been traced in his theory of soul. "The soul is a fine substance distributed through the whole mass of body, and most resembles the air with an infusion of warmth." In view of the fact that Epicuros reduces the atoms to the smallest uniform size, his "soul-substance" may not appear as material as the "soul-atoms" of Democritos. But both are equally subject to the same mechanical motion governing matter. Besides, while talking of the soul, Epicuros makes it quite clear that it is neither immaterial nor simple nor immortal. Epicurean soul dies with the body. Therefore, it is obviously the vital phenomenon which is produced by a certain combination of matter. When nothing was known regarding the nerve-force, some differentiation of matter had to be assumed for the explanation of life. But that by no means admits the existence of a non-material spirit parallel to, and independent of, matter.

The most advanced section of mankind boldly freed itself from the awe of natural phenomena. It dared look nature in the face; tore off her veil of mystery; and set aside the mythical gods. It wanted to know the causes of the phenomena of nature, and sought them in the nature itself. Thus philosophy was born.

But to undertake a task is yet far from accomplishing it. To know nature, man must overcome nature. Knowledge is acquired not through contemplation, but action. No amount of argumentation would convince one of the sweetness of sugar, unless he ate it. Philosophy degenerated into metaphysics, because man was not yet sufficiently advanced in his conquest of nature. The materialist conception of the origin and evolution of the Universe is the mother of science. Unless a thing is assumed to be knowable, efforts to know it cannot begin. The rational cosmological conception of the philosophers of ancient Greece sowed the seeds of science. The materialist philosophy gave birth to science; in its turn, it could be victorious only on the basis of scientific knowledge. The grand mission of knowing nature in order to explain its diverse phenomena in physical terms, set before mankind in its early youth, could not be accomplished by one man, nor in one generation, nor even in an entire age. It is the mission of mankind; the history of mankind is the record of the realisation of this mission. The progressive accomplishment of the mission being conditional upon the conquest of nature, materialism, apparently overwhelmed by metaphysics, reappeared in the field of human ideology as soon as experimental science began to develop. Each great discovery of modern science strengthened the foundation of materialism. But even in the antique period, materialism was overwhelmed only apparently.

The materialist cosmology of Democritos, improved by Epicuros, survived Christian theology and scholastic metaphysics which drew inspiration from Plato, Aristotle and the Stoics. The rational materialistic foundation of the Aristotelian system itself eventually shook off its metaphysical super-structure, to become a powerful lever of modern civilisation. At the close of the middle-ages, the rationalist Aristotle deposed the master of metaphysics who had dominated European thought for more than a thousand years.

The metaphysical deviation of the Greek philosophy led up to the establishment of the Catholic Church which held European humanity in ignorance and superstition, and therefore obstructed all spiritual progress for so many hundred years. But at the same time, its materialist essence promoted the scientific culture of Alexandria. An outcome of the Democritan and Epicurean conception of the uniformity and necessity in the course of nature, Alexandrian learning was the brilliant prelude to the age of modern science, though separated from the latter by more than one thousand and five hundred years. As a matter of fact, Copernicus, Galileo, Kepler and Newton took up the thread of science left off by Archimedes, Aristarchos, Hypparchos, Euclid and others. Even in organic science, Galen was not far behind the point from which Lamarck and Darwin began. Thus, fifteen hundred years of metaphysics and theology could not deprive humanity of its materialist heritage. As soon as social conditions enabled European humanity to return to the conquest of nature, a process disturbed by the chaos following the decline and downfall of the Roman Empire, the fire of knowledge, kindled in antiquity, began to shine through the darkness of faith.

To testify the spiritual role of materialism, no better evidence could be adduced than that of the German scholar Albert Lange, who wrote a monumental history of materialism with the object of refuting it—but unsuccessfully.

"Greek philosophy, springing from a materialistic origin, after a short and brilliant passage through all conceivable standpoints, found its termination in materialistic systems and materialistic modifications of other systems....If by practical materialism we understand a dominant inclination to material acquisition and enjoyment, then, theoretical materialism is opposed to it, as is every effort of the spirit towards knowledge. Nay, we may say that the sober earnest which marks the great materialist systems of antiquity is perhaps more suited than an enthusiastic Idealism, which only too easily results in its own bewilderment, to keep the soul clear of all that is low and vulgar, and to lend it a lasting effort after worthy objects."

What is said here about ancient materialism, is applicable all the more to the modern materialist philosophy. For, the latter, based upon the general principle propounded at the birth of philosophy, is no longer a hypothesis, but a conclusively verified cosmological conception which opens up before man an endless perspective of continuous progress.

What, vulgarly or by mistake, is taken for materialism, and so sanctimoniously condemned by its opponents—religionists, spiritualists, idealists etc.—has nothing to do with the materialist philosophy. Indeed, it is the very essence of religion which is materialist in the worst sense of the term. Egoism induces man either to pray for his daily bread or to strive for the salvation of his soul. The doctrine of super-natural creation is the basis of all religion. This doctrine glorifies unbounded egoism as the attribute of the God or the property of the Final Cause. The world is either the product of the arbitrary will of an all-powerful, that is, irresponsible God, or a permanent miracle—something growing out of nothing. The world has no being in itself and by itself. Product of an arbitrary or miraculous act, it is always governed by arbitrary laws which, in the last analysis, can mean only the expression of an unbounded ego. The supreme egoism of religion reaches the climax in Hinduism,* which paradoxically claims to be the most spiritual of all religions. According to it, the creation is the play of God. The object of human devotion, which is assumed to be the reservoir of all ideals, is the greatest egoist conceivable. For his own pleasure, he plays with worlds and with the fate of men. The God is the personification of power, absolute and unrestricted, created after the image of the man of elemental desires and ambitions. He is arrogant, arbitrary, merciless, lusting for power. Believers in such a "divine ruler" or "spiritual principle" are necessarily adepts to the egoistic dictum: Each for himself, devil takes the hindmost. Helpless playthings of an unbounded and irresponsible Ego, man can have no other ideal than to save himself. The much applauded virtue of renunciation is the supreme form of selfishness. It simply means to

* A Panegyrist of "Indo-Aryan spirituality", like Havell, finds the Vedic religion to be "gross materialism."

save your own precious self, the rest of the world may go to the devil.

The religious man's view of nature is purely utilitarian. In the beginning, he worships (not from devotion, but from fear) the imaginary gods so that he may get all he wants. The ideal of Heaven, be it of the Hindus, Moslems or Christians, makes the most fastidious bon-vivant's mouth water. Later on, the religious man looks upon nature as a dark, evil, passive thing which becomes the world only for himself, either as the bounty of God, as the reward for the religious, or as a gratuitous stage-setting for the soul to perform the magic of bursting an imaginary chain.

For the materialist, in contrast, nature exists by itself—not to satisfy man's egoism, but to be admired, observed, investigated and known by man, himself a product of nature. In this attitude towards nature lies the root of all the noble qualities of man which materialism is supposed to kill. The holy man, who deplores the perversities of the wicked world, retires on the altitude of his "spiritual" egoism to save himself from the deadly contagion. But a scientist, who may not believe in any God, cheerfully and without the arrogance of a holy egoist, sacrifices his life for the benefit of the world. The supreme selfishness of deserting the ship because it appears in one's dream to be in flames, is foreign to materialism which does not find fault with the world, but accepts it as it is with the object of improving it. The materialist philosophy does not passively interpret the world and impotently bewail its defects. It shows the way to rebuild it.

While religion binds man in his own petty egoism, the human spirit finds unrestricted freedom in materialism. Man goes beyond the narrow limits of his self only when he gets over the idea of supernatural creation, and is able to look upon nature as existing by itself in all its beauty, grandeur and potentialities. Only then, he merges his self in the universal being. The religious man's morality is either hypocrisy, or performed under duress. The materialist is moral by his own conviction. He practises virtue not as payment for a place in Heaven or for the salvation of his soul, but simply because he cannot help it. His conception of man as an infinitesimal particle in the grand scheme of the Cosmos makes absolutely no room for egoism.

# CHAPTER III

## MATERIALISM IN INDIAN PHILOSOPHY

IN INDIA also, the dissatisfaction with the Vedic Natural Religion gave rise to speculations about the origin of things. Some of the earlier Upanishads are fragmentary records of those speculations. But for reasons stated in the preceding chapter, early Indian speculations about the origin of things developed directly into metaphysics and a precarious form of monotheistic religion. Yet, towards the close of the misty Vedic era, approximately about the nineth or eighth century B.C., there rose thinkers who represented distinct materialist tendencies. The teachings of those early speculative rebels are almost completely lost. Only the general drift of the currents of their thought can be approximately inferred from the works of their orthodox opponents. There is, however, ample evidence to conclude that the too earlier systems of Hindu philosophy—Vaisheshik and Sankhya—were the positive outcome of the speculations recorded fragmentarily and rather enigmatically in the earlier Upanishads. The Vedic society was in the process of dissolution. The pastoral tribal organisation, under priestly domination, was buttressed ideologically on the natural religion of the Vedas. The ideology of the forces making for its dissolution was expressed by the philosophers who challenged the authority of the gods by trying to explain the being and becoming of the world in a rationalist and materialist way.

All the existing schools of philosophy mention earlier thinkers as "heretics" or "nihilists". The former had denied the authority of the Vedas; the latter doubted if anything existed at all. According to the Sankhyas, the "nihilists" held: "Since nothing really exists, except thought, neither does bondage exist; just as the things of a dream have no real existence. Therefore, it (bondage) has no cause; for it is absolutely false. The reality is a void. What is, perishes, because to perish is the habit of things. The void alone is the reality. Since everything that exists, perishes, and that which is perishable is false, as in a dream, bondage has merely a momentary existence, is phenomenal, and not real. Therefore, who can be bound by that? Nothing continues after quitting its own nature; therefore, nothing could continue in existence, if it ceased to perish (that is, ceased to have its nature)."

From such fragmentary records, it is very difficult to reconstruct the whole system. But to do so, obviously is essential for the composition of a complete history of ancient Indian thought. For the moment, the fragmentary evidence clearly proves that the speculative efforts made to outgrow the childishness of the Vedic Natural Religion did not directly develop into the metaphysical conceptions recorded in the existing Upanishads. There was a distinct tendency of development in the opposite direction. Not only was the authority of the Vedas boldly challenged, but the earlier forms of metaphysical thought were subjected to ridicule, and the denial of the Gods or supernatural agencies was stretched to the logical conclusion of denying the existence of everything since this latter depended on the existence of imaginary metaphysical entities.

Nihilism was the ideology of the dissolution of antique society in India. It was revolutionary in the sense that it was a mighty revolt against Vedic priestcraft; but as a school of philosophical thought, it was sterile. Nevertheless, it was so powerful that subsequently it very greatly influenced Buddhist philosophy. The nihilist must have been very powerful, because all the philosophical schools developed for disputing the nihilist doctrine. The materialist schools of Indian philosophy represented currents of thought evidently stimulated by nihilism. In order to dispute the doctrine that nothing existed, it was necessary to rely upon the existence of the material world which no sensible person could possibly dispute. The connection between nihilism and the outspokenly materialistic Vaisheshik system still remains a matter of investigation. But its connection with the quasi-materialist Sankhya system is quite evident. In their fight against the nihilists, the Sankhyas were driven very close to out and out materialism. In order to prove the reality of some existence, Kapila had to fall back upon the material world. The existence of thought by itself, or that of disembodied spirits, could not be proved to the satisfaction of the sceptics who expounded their nihilist doctrines as the logical deductions from the early spiritualist cult which was being set up in order to drug the victims of social chaos, so that they might ignore the miseries of this world as bad dreams. Therefore, more tangible evidence for the reality of existence had to be produced. The rebels and revolutionaries of ancient India thus made the rise of a philosophy possible. In order to prove the existence of thought, Kapila, for example, had to refer the reality of thought to the reality of the external world. His highly materialistic theory of cognition was also developed under the powerful impact of nihilism.

Even in the major Upanishads, which have come to be regarded as the foundation of the Vedantist metaphysical system, the discerning student finds unmistakable evidence of materialism. That is only natural; because the speculations of men, whose spiritual thirst is no longer satisfied with the moonshine of natural religion, inevitably tends towards a physical explanation of natural phenomena. Ancient Indian speculation could not be free from this general psychological rule. Fragmentary evidence only proves that records of the early materialistic thought were destroyed in course of time. Until those lost chapters of the spiritual history of India are recovered or re-written, Indian philosophy will hang in the air. Pending the accomplishment of that outstanding task, for the present purpose it will be sufficient to reproduce some well known passages from the more important Upanishads:

"What is the origin of the world? Ether, (akash), for all these beings take their rise from ether only, and return into ether. Ether is their rest."

Again, "That which is called ether, is the revealer of all forms and names."*

If the conception of *akash* is devoid of all content, then, the argument of the nihilists becomes unanswerable, and everything must be reduced to nothing, as non-existent. Moreover, in the same Upanishada, Brahman is also mentioned as the cause of everything. If *akash* was a metaphysical conception, identical with Brahman, it would not be necessary for its being specified as the revealer of all forms and names, in addition to Brahman. Obviously, the function of revealing forms and names does not belong to Brahman. If things are supposed to have another cause, over and above the metaphysical Final Cause, then, the former must logically be conceived as a material cause. There must have been dispute on this point. Because Sankaracharya found it necessary to insist that "the word ether must here be taken to denote Brahman." But it is equally, or perhaps more, logical to assume that the obvious meaning of the passage is more sensible and, in that case, the fact that Brahman also was mentioned as the cause of all is to be set to the credit of prevailing prejudice. The assumption of the material cause, named ether, is sufficient for explaining the origin of the world. Yet, the venerable conception of Brahman is retained as a matter of form. The entire history of scientific thought, almost down to our days, suffers from this fallacy.

In the Katha Upanishad, the world is visualised as evolving out of a primal material condition. Kapila takes that as his point of departure for the

* Tchandogya Upanishad.

doctrine of the Pradhan and Avyakta (undeveloped or potential.)

In Svetasvatara Upanishad, Aga (fire) is assumed as "the one unborn from which everything springs". Aga is not, however, identified with Brahman. So, it must have been conceived as a cause other than the spiritual First Cause. Here again, the physical world is traced to a material origin. The materialistic tendency in the Svetasvatara Upanishad is so very pronounced that even Sankaracharya finds it very difficult to explain it away. It will be shown later on that, in order to combat Buddhism which was the ultimate outcome of all the materialist tendencies in ancient India, Sankaracharya was compelled to take up a very thinly veiled materialistic position.

The Vedanta has come to be accepted as the most representative and authoritative school of ancient Indian philosophy. As its name implies, it claims to contain all the wisdom of the Vedas. But being based on the authority of the Scriptures, it can hardly be accorded the distinction of philosophy. As a matter of fact, Vedanta is a very highly metaphysical system of theology. As such, it goes beyond the limits of a theistic religion, and represents a very highly developed form of pantheism. Pantheism is only inverted materialism. No other logical conclusion can be drawn from any consistent system of monism. The Vedantist metaphysical speculation completely destroys the idea of a god, and consequently liquidates religion. The materialist implication of the Vedantist pantheism becomes evident in its masterly exposition by Sankaracharya. The metaphysical monism of the Vedanta system was constructed by the Brahmin intellectuals in order to combat the materialist schools of philosophy which had logically resulted from the earlier speculation of thinkers no longer satisfied with the fantasies and fairy-tales of the primitive Vedic religion.

The spiritual revolt represented by the Indian materialists eventually culminated in the rise of Buddhism which all but liquidated the Vedic natural religion and freed India from Brahmanical domination for several hundred years. Internal evidence proves that the Vedanta Sutras were composed for combating Buddhism. Therefore, they could not be regarded as the direct outcome of the speculative thought recorded in the Upanishads. The composition of the earlier Upanishads and the Vedanta Sutras must have been separated by seviral hundred years, during which period the spiritual development of India was in the direction of materialism, represented by Kanada, Kapila and many others, and of rationalism, represented by the Buddhists and Jains subsequently. The triumph of Buddhism, and its supremacy for so many centuries prove that the metaphysical school of thought, represented by the Vedantists, could not check the tide of materialism and rationalism. It was only after the defeat of the Buddhist revolution that Vedantist metaphysics and pantheism were revived as the ideology of the Brahmanical reaction. The Sutras themselves could not have been compiled earlier than the fourth century B.C., by which time Buddhism had become a powerful challenge to the

Brahmanical orthodoxy. Because, a considerable portion of them is devoted to a vigorous polemic against the Buddhists. On the other hand, the philosophical origin of Buddhism is clearly to be traced to the Sankhya and Vaisheshik systems. The early Buddhist as well as Jain philosophers drew their inspiration from Kanada and Kapila.

Although there is reason to believe that those fathers of Hindu philosophy lived more or less at the same time, a comparative study of the two systems allows the inference that Vaisheshik was the oldest system of Hindu philosophy. Its founder lived about the same time as the founder of ancient Greek materialism, namely, approximately, in the eighth century B.C. He also expounded an atomist theory for explaining the origin of the world. The following are the main points of Kanada's atomism.

All substance is composed of parts which are governed by their qualities of inherence and conjunction. That thing at which the distinction of whole and the parts stops, and which therefore marks the limit of division into minuter parts, is the atom. The atoms are the cause of the world; an effect may not be assumed without cause. The atoms are eternal, belong to four classes which possess corresponding qualities. The atoms of the same class and of similar quality combine to produce the several gross elements. The combination takes place by two causes: The material cause, inherent in the atoms themselves, and the non-inherent cause is assumed to be the super-natural will.

All substances consisting of parts originate from the substances connected with them by the relation of inherence. The substance is composed of parts inherent in it. The relation of conjunction operated in the process. Inherent parts of a substance come together, thanks to the relation of conjunction, to produce the substance. Whatever consists of parts, originates from those substances with which it is connected by the relation of inherence, conjunction co-operating. The whole world is composed of parts; because it is composed of parts, it has beginning and end; an effect may not be assumed without a cause; therefore, the atoms are the cause of the world. The atoms are of a spherical shape. When the atoms are isolated and motionless, no effect is produced. After that, the unseen principle, acting as the operative cause, and conjunction co-operating, they produce the entire aggregate of things, beginning with binary atoms. The material cause of the atomic compound is the constituent atoms; the conjunction is caused by the unseen operative cause.

The materialism of the system is evident. The only weak spot in an otherwise self-contained system of purely physical explanation of the origin of the world, is the assumption of the unseen, non-inherent, cause in addition to the material cause. Obviously, the assumption is superfluous. Since the tendency to combine is inherent in atoms themselves, there is absolutely no need for an unseen (adrishta) cause to make them coalesce. The Vaisheshik system does not need an impulse from outside for the atoms to begin aggregating. The tendency to combine is inherent in the atoms. "Bigness is produced from plurality inherent in the causes." That is to say, to combine is in the nature of the atoms. Kanad himself did not go so far as to visualise his atoms in a perpetual motion. The postulation of a motionless state of isolated atoms required the additional postulate of the action of the "unseen principle". The commentator Upaskar removes the defect. According to him, extension, that is, perceptible matter, is caused by the principle of "dvitva" inherent in the primal matter; it is a natural propensity of two atoms to unite. Indeed, the commentator makes clear an idea to be found in the Sutras themselves.

However, in assuming the superfluous non-inherent cause, Kanad did not contradict himself any more crassly than did, much later, the fathers of modern science like Copernicus, Galileo, Descartes, Newton and others who paid homage to the prejudice about God, even when they deprived him of all functions. To-day it is not possible to say whether Kanad himself believed or not in the necessity of the obviously superfluous assumption of the non-inherent cause. Even if he did, that would not affect the real implication of his hypothesis, which was purely materialistic.

Kanad's system makes no room for the soul in the metaphysical or spiritualist sense of the term. According to it, intelligence is not an inherent property of the soul; it is conceived as a mere adventitious quality of the atoms, arising only when the soul is joined with an internal organ. Kanad argues: The qualities which inhere in the substance, constituting the cause, originate qualities of the same kind in the substance constituting the effect. Hence, if the intelligent Brahman is assumed as the cause of the world, we should expect to find intelligence inherent in the effect also, in the world. This is not the case. Therefore, Brahman cannot be the cause of the world. Consciousness is thus regarded as the product of a complicated combination of atoms. Soul is merely the disposition of organism, which is a combination of matter. At a certain stage of combination, an atomic aggregate acquires the property of receiving impressions of external objects and reacting to them. Consciousness develops at that stage. The constituents of the "soul" of the Vaisheshik system are inherent in the substance which constitutes the organism. And that substance is composed of atoms, which again are only of four kinds —of water, earth, air and fire.

Moreover, while disputing the immateriality of spirituality of the soul, Kanad himself throws overboard the superfluous assumption of the non-inherent cause. He categorically declares that the Brahman cannot be the cause of the world. And in another place, he declares equally categorically that the atoms are the cause of the world. The early Indian metaphysicians regarded Brahman as in intelligent being or an intelligent principle. The materialists combated that conception. They could do so because they did not require the postulate of an external intelligence or force to give the first impulse for the origin of the world. Therefore, their materialist speculation was self-contained, the formal inclusion of the conception of Brahman or non-inherent cause was only a matter of prejudice or conformity with venerable traditions.

The Vaisheshik system was condemned by the

orthodox as "semi-destructive" or "semi-nihilistic", because of its dialectic dynamic view of nature. It regards nature not as a being but a process of becoming. It held that the continuous change in the size of bodies involved continuous perishing of the old and continuous rise of new substance. Even the idea of the indestructibility of matter is anticipated.

As a matter of fact, Kanada's atomism was even more self-contained than that of Democritos. By visualising the atoms as possessing the inherent property of coalescing and combining, it was free from the fallacy which opened the Democritean system to Aristotle's attack. Kanada's system was to a large extent free from the problem of action at a distance. In his time, it was the dominating current of thought. The Vaisheshik atomism was the common point of departure of a whole series of speculative thinkers, whose contributions to the spiritual heritage of India approximated real philosophy, and tried to free Indian society from the domination of the Vedic priestcraft. Nevertheless, the unnecessary assumption of a metaphysical cause was due to the priestly prejudices from which the main currents of materialist and rationalist thought in ancient India could not liberate themselves. The social conditions that caused in Greece the evolution of thought from natural religion to the materialist philosophy, did not ripen in India. Intellectual life remained a priestly monopoly. The result was the weakness of the scientific and rationalist thought which, therefore, was eventually overwhelmed and even its records were practically all destroyed by the triumphant Brahmanical reaction.

Although the fundamental principles of ancient Indian materialism were stated originally in the Vaisheshik system, the dominating position in the intellectual life of that period came to be occupied by the Sankhya system of Kapila. The latter deviated largely from the strictly materialistic ground, and developed rather as a rational-naturalist system of metaphysics. Nevertheless, the physical principles of materialism were elaborated philosophically by Kapila. He is known as an atheist who maintained that the existence of God could not be proved by logical evidence. But the real merit of his philosophy is the recognition of the objective reality of the physical world. The Sankhya system decidedly rejects the doctrine that the external world has no objective existence, and that nothing exists but thought. Arguing against some earlier philosophers, who are characterised by the commentators as "heretics" or "nihilists", Kapila lays down: "Not thought alone exists; because there is the intuition of the external world."

"Then, since, if the one does not exist, the other does not exist, there is a void."*

The most authoritative commentator, Vijnana Bhikshu, interprets the Sutras as follows: "The reality is not thought alone; because external objects also are proved to exist, just as thought is, by intuition. If external things do not exist, then, a mere void offers itself. Because, if the external world does not exist, then, thought does not exist; for, it is intuition that proves the objective; and, if the in-

* Book I, Sutras 42 and 43.

tuition of the external did not establish the objective, then, the intuition of thought also would not establish the existence of thought."

The anology with the point of departure of Descartes' rationalism—Cogito, ergo sum—is obvious. But there is more than pure rationalism. The theory of cognition is definitely materialistic. The underlying principle of the Sankhya theory of knowledge is identical with the modern materialist principle that consciousness is determined by being. The defenders of the religious doctrine of creation tried to silence the enquiry about the origin of things by denying the reality of the world itself. They argued that a thing of dream—an unreality—did not need a substantial origin. Kapila retorted: "The world is not unreal; because there is no fact contradictory (to its reality), and because it is not the (false) result of depraved senses (leading to a belief in what ought not to be believed)." This is clear enough. But Kapila goes farther—to the extent of stating the fundamental principle of the rationalist-materialist view of the world.

"A thing is not made out of nothing."* The bottom is knocked off the doctrine of creation. The origin of the physical world is traced to an endless process of causality, and that process is inherent in nature. Existing eternally by itself, the world does not need a creator or creation. Nor is there any beginning. Because, in that case also, something would come out of nothing. Thus, the Sankhya system rejects even "emanent teleology", a doctrine made fashionable by some philosophers of our time.

* Book I, Sutras 78.

The materialist essence of the Sankhya system is confused by its apparent rejection of atomism. But the very argument advanced for the purpose implies a more perfected form of materialism: "What is limited, cannot be the substance of all." Together with the Vaisheshik, the Sankhya system also reduces the "gross elements" to atoms; but Kapila traces the severally existing atoms down to a still simpler all-pervading existence. This is very much the same as done by Aristotle: but there is no evidence whether he resorted to this expediency to avoid the baffling problem of action at a distance. However, by seeking the ultimate substance beyond the atoms, Kapila anticipated the most modern conception of substance instead of rejecting materialism.

Kapila visualised existence as a hierarchy, so to say, composed of twenty-five realities. In addition to the soul, nature, mind and self-consciousness, there are "subtle" elements, sense organs and "gross elements". The pyramid stands on the apex. Reverse the order, and you have a process of evolution. But Kapila conceived the process on the Hegelian fashion as "Idea expressing itself". Although the process of evolution is set on its head, the "realities", however, are derived inductively from the immediately perceptible gross elements. The existence of the "subtle elements" (sound, colour, touch, taste and smell) is inferred from the "gross elements" which are directly perceptible. The logic is obvious: Everything that is gross, is formed of something which is less gross. The process is traced to the primal state of nature in which everything lies in a state of inaction. But Nature is not only eternal, but self-operative. "Since the root has no root, the root is rootless."* Thus, Nature is the Final Cause. Since mind and self-consciousness are placed within the scheme of nature, they are included in the materialistic system. Only the soul stands outside, but like Newton's *deux ex machina,* it is completely unnecessary for explaining the being and becoming of the world. The existence of nature is inferred from its perceptible phenomena. These are real; they must therefore have a real cause. That is to say, the constituents of the world exist eternally. Those ultimate elements are called, in the Vaisheshik and Nyaya systems, atoms. Kapila reduces them to an all-pervasive existence, and calls it the nature in a state of inaction.

The Sankhya nature in its primal state is like Spinoza's "beseelte Materie" (animated substance). Three qualities (goodness, passion and darkness), inherent in nature, are the lever of all natural operations. Atomism is rejected, because pain and pleasure are not properties of the atom. Everything in existence is an aggregate of pain, pleasure, delusion etc. which are clearly perceptible. But here arises a very pertinent question: What is the cause of these categories or qualities? Kapila himself asserts that something cannot come out of nothing. Obviously to avoid this dilemma, he makes his Nature an all-pervading primal substance, having the three qualities in a state of equilibrium. The atomists would contend that the atom could just as well represent the equilibrium of qualities. However, Kapila's rejection of atomism leads him to a

* Book I, Sutras 114 and 115.

position where the materialness of nature appears to disappear. The primal existence appears like the Brahman of the Vedantist, or the Hegelian Non-Being—Absolute Nothing. But that is far from what Kapila desires to establish. Therefore, he concludes his arguments against atomism by reaffirming the materialness of nature.

"Nothing can be produced from a non-entity like man's horn."

"There must be some material of which the product may consist."*

The Sankhya system, with its rigid rationalism, cannot do without a material substratum of the world. Because, if that is dispensed with, everything may happen everywhere, which is an absurdity according to itself. Consequently, the Sankhya conception of primal nature cannot be essentially different from the latter conception of "matter in motion". Its rejection of atomism, therefore, could not be a repudiation of materialism; it was done with the motive of making the physical explanation of the world free from all possible logical fallacies. An all-pervasive primal substance obviates the difficulty of original combination, and consequently, for securing the first impulse, the postulate of a metaphysical agency is not necessary.

Indeed, a mechanistic conception of nature is not only logically inherent in the Sankhya system, but becomes explicit in the definition of the properties of the "*Pradhan*". Kapila holds that just as mother's milk and water flow mechanically, just so

* Book I, Sutras 114 and 115.

"the *Pradhan* also, although non-intelligent, may be supposed to move from its own nature." Motion, as distinct from conscious movement or intelligence, is thus clearly visualised as inherent in the *Pradhan*, which is the name for the all-pervading material substratum of the world. This again shows that the metaphysical elements in the Sankhya system are altogether superfluous, the system being self-contained as a mechanistic-materialist conception of the world.

As regards the soul, it is explicitly ruled out as the Final Cause of things; and the obvious logical deduction that the origin of things is material is clearly drawn from the superfluity of the conception of soul.

"While both (Nature and Soul) are antecedent (to all products), since the one (Soul) is devoid (of this character of being a cause), it is applicable only to the other of the two (Nature)."*

Having divested soul of all qualities, and ascribed to nature all active properties and the status of the Final Cause, Kapila finds it very difficult to prove how the non-discrimination between the two originates. The difficulty lies in the fact that his conception of the Nature as a self-operative entity renders soul only an empty conception,—a concession to traditional prejudice. He extricates himself from the position by going still another step farther away from metaphysical dualism towards materialistic monism. Understanding, mind, reason, and even ego, are all discriminated from the

* Book I, Sutras 75.

Soul as products of Nature. Thus, the Soul is left without any function. Indeed, by its very nature (absolute, immutable etc.), it cannot have any connection with anything. Thus, there is an unbridgeable gulf between the two ultimate categories of existence. The gulf could be bridged only by abandoning the dualist position. It is difficult to ascertain if Kapila himself did that. The Sutras are not very clear on the point. One of the commentators cuts the Gordian knot.

"These two (Nature and Soul) are alike without antecedent, like seed and sprout of which it is needless to ask which is the first; the old puzzle, which was the first, the acorn or the oak? being a frivolous question."

The relation between Soul and Nature (*prakriti* and *purusha*) thus interpreted, the Sankhya becomes free of the dualist fallacy, and stands out as a self-contained materialist system. Either simultaneous existence of the two uncreated beings is admitted, or Soul ceased to exist except as an attribute of Nature. Then, the logic of "seed and sprout" is faulty. The removal of this logical defect leads to monism. Of the Soul and Nature, one must be the cause of the other. By its very nature, the Soul of Sankhya can not be the cause of creation; because, in that case, it would cease to be what it is and could never be emancipated. So, there remains only Nature as the only real source of existence, and Kapila conceives Nature as a purely material entity, self-originating and functioning mechanically. Even the so-called vital forces are the products of the mechanistic operation of the material entity Nature.

The most important contribution made to the development of philosophical thought by the Sankhya system, however, is its sensationalist theory of knowledge. Kapila was an out and out empiricist. He holds, with an admirable logical rigour, that sense perception is the only reliable source of knowledge.

"Determination (right apprehension) of something not previously known is right notion (knowledge). What is in the highest degree productive thereof, is evidence."*

Evidence is defined as perception, inference and testimony (scriptural). By admitting inference in the category of evidence, Kapila anticipated the rise of inductive logic. His contribution to the scientific mode of thought, therefore, is very considerable. The above Sutra is interpreted by one of the commentators as follows: "The proof or evidence, or whatever we may choose to call that from which right notion results, is just the conjunction of an organ (with the appropriate object)."

The Sutras themselves are very categorical about the role of perception in the process of acquiring knowledge. A decisive answer to the questions raised even by modern epistemological nihilists was given by Kapila.

"Perception is that discernment which, being in conjunction (with the things perceived), portrays the forms thereof."

It is held that the organs (external, that is, of

* Book I, Sutras 87.

† Book 1, Sutras 89.

perception, and internal, that is, of inference) are products of Nature. They are not "depraved"; that is, they do not portray as real what is not real. Therefore, whatever is established on their evidence, is real. Since the organs bear testimony to the existence of the external world, its reality is established.

As the composite outcome of all the positive elements in the whole previous history of Indian thought, Buddhism shook the very foundation of the hoary edifice of Brahmanical orthodoxy. It disputed the authority of the Scriptures; vigorously condemned the sacrificial rites and rituals of the Vedic Natural Religion; it denied the existence even of an impersonal First Cause (the Brahman of the Upanishads); and is discarded the doctrine of Soul. For the first time, there began to develop in India a system of truly philosophical thought, having for its point of departure the atomism of the Vaisheshik system and the rationalist-mechanistic conception of Nature contained in the Sankhya system.

Moreover, the Buddhist philosophers, particularly of the "realist" (*Sarvastitvavadins*) and the "nihilist" (*Sunyavadins*) schools, took over the sceptical views of the earliest ideological rebels who preceded the formulation of the materialist systems of the Vaisheshiks and Sankhyas. But the so-called "nihilism" of the Buddhists is to be traced back directly to the dialectic view of nature that the continuous change in bodies, owing to atomic combination and separation, necessarily involves a continuous process of the old perishing and the new growing. This dynamic view of nature was formulated in the Vaisheshik system, and subsequently elaborated by Kapila, who, notwithstanding his unnecessary metaphysical deviation, was essentially a materialist.

The Buddhist "nihilists", however, did not reduce everything to non-existence as had been done by the older nihilists. The Buddhists visualised everything in an endless process of constant flux. They challenged the notion of an eternal, changeless, absolute existence. The logical consequence of their dynamic view was the rejection of the dogma of the Absolute Truth revealed in the Vedas. All the three schools of the Buddhist philosophy (including the Idealists—*Vijnanvadins*) taught that every existence is momentary—in a state of eternal flux. Their doctrine controverted the basic assumption of the orthodox Hindu philosophy of the Vedanta system.

On the basis of the materialistic and quasi-materialistic Vaisheshik and Sankhya systems, Buddha reversed the relation between the spiritual and material beings. As a consequence of the reversal of the order of sequence, their relative values were also revaluated. Buddha held that soul is a bye-product of the very being of man, governed by the laws of nature. Thus differentiated from, and contrasted with, "the spiritual", being could only mean physical being. The Buddhist conception of individual consciousness does not carry with it any assertion or implication that "I" exist, or am in any way a reality. What really exists, according to Buddhism, is "sanskaras"—activities and impressions man receives in course of these activities. The "sanskaras", again, work out in a casual series. The metaphysical dogma of the freedom of will necessarily disappears with the soul. The soul does not inspire the activities of man's life; on the contrary, it is the sum total of impressions accumulated by organic activities.

The materialist essence of Buddhist philosophy, although couched in an ethico-idealistic terminology, stands out in a clear relief under the fierce attack of its Brahmanical opponents. Sankaracharya, for example, exclaimed in exasperation: "Thus, blind karma is permanent, having the power to produce an infinite number of conscious individuals—souls!" A correct evaluation of consciousness, which implied devaluation of the soul, the denial of its spiritual nature, and precedence over physical being, led Buddha to do away with the belief in God, who can be conceived *philosophically* only as the "Universal Soul". For the solution of the question of life, Buddha found that belief in God was useless. Since the existence of God, as the spiritual cause of the Universe, can be established only upon the assumption of the extra-materiality of human consciousness, the rejection of the doctrine of soul necessarily leads to the denial of God. God cannot be reached except through the doctrine of soul.

The Realist school of Buddhism defines the existence of a thing as its causal efficiency. According to this essentially materialistic doctrine, the existence of an abstract principle cannot be proved. The Nihilist school is deduced from the Realist. It holds that, since everything is being constantly destroyed, a void—non-existence—is the cause of everything. According to Sankaracharya, they preached the following doctrine: "Nothing can become a cause as long as it remains unchanged, but has to that end undergo destruction, and that thus existence springs from non-existence only". The Buddhist Sutra itself is: "On account of the manifestation (of effects) not without previous destruction (of the cause)." The seed must decompose, become non-existent *as seed,* before the plant can grow. The world is thus visualised as a self-originating, dynamic process. There is no difference between the Realists and the Nihilists, if their common materialist essence is divested of scholastic sophistry.

Buddhist materialism was based on Vaisheshik atomism. It can be summarised as follows: There are two aggregates of existence—external (material) and internal (mental). But mind presupposes the existence of an atomic combination. The external, composed of the "elements" (*bhuta*) and "elementals" (*bhautika*), embrace the outside nature as well as the gross bodily organs. The former is made of elements which are earth, water, fire and air. These, in their turn, are formed respectively of the different kinds of atoms; whereas the latter are made of the "elementals", that is, diverse combinations of the elements.

Since mind and things mental are conditional upon the existence of an atomic aggregate, the "internal" is evidently not an independent being; it grows out of the "external". In other words, the mental is derived from the material. This is further evidenced from the division of the "internal" into five groups (*skandhas*). They are sensation, knowledge, feeling, verbal knowledge and impression. These are all diverse functions of the bodily organism—an aggregate of atoms. No school of Buddhist philosophy admits the existence of any extra-natural or metaphysical intelligence, such as God or Soul, which might bring about the first aggregation of atoms. Therefore, atomic combination must be visualised as a mechanical process out of which the so-called "internal", that is, the intelligent part of existence, arises.

But the Buddhist philosophy stopped short of this logical conclusion from its own premises. The reason of that short-coming was the idea of "*Nirwana*", which was the characteristic feature of a psychological condition created in an atmosphere of social dissolution. The world is full of sorrows and miseries. One must run away from it. But the cardinal principle of Buddhism, namely, "*Nirwana*", contradicted the entire system of Buddhist philosophy. Sankaracharya pointed out that contradiction. "Nor can the atom and *skandhas* be assumed to enter on activity on their own account, for that would imply their never ceasing to be active." The ideal of "*Nirwana*" is the cessation of all activity. According to the Buddhist mechanistic view of nature, atoms and their aggregates are auto-active. Therefore, as Sankaracharya pointed out, their activity can never cease. The material world is eternal.

The ideal of "*Nirwana*" represented the nihilism of Buddhist philosophy. It was the quintessence of the ideology of social dissolution. The positive materialist character of Buddhism made it victorious, for a time. But eventually, it was bound to be overwhelmed by its own contradictions. Buddhism was the product of the social conditions of the epoch. It was the ideology of those who could not deny the effects (pains etc.) of the material existence. For the multitude, the conditions of social dissolution only meant pains. So, that was the effect of their material existence. On the other hand, the initial triumph of Buddhism was due to the fact that it secured the adhesion of a rising class which rejected the Brahmanic dogma of other-worldliness. According to Sankaracharya, Buddha himself was an idealist. Nevertheless, he propounded a realistic philosophy, "conforming himself to the mental state of some of his disciples." It is recorded that hundreds of merchants were associated with Gautama.

The idealistic deviation of the Buddhist philosophy was caused by its having enlisted the patronage of the upper classes. In order to refute the Brahmanical dogma of the Eternal Truth, the rebels expounded the doctrine of the momentariness of everything. In course of time, the doctrine of temporariness was applied not only to the physical, but also to the mental phenomena. The adverse effects of the social existence, pain, sorrow, etc., were also declared to be momentary. One step farther, and Buddhist philosophy shifted its moorings from materialism to idealism. What is momentary, is not real; therefore, pain etc. are but ideas which have no objective causes. They are only mental states. There does not exist anything but ideas. But the other cardinal principle of the Buddhist philosophy could not be altogether discarded. The phenomenal world is without a beginning. But ideas also have always existed in a chain of mutual causality. They do not need any external object. They are self-existing.

That reaction of Buddhist philosophy reflected the interest of ruling classes which wished to arrest the process of social dissolution. The idealist deviation rendered Buddhism susceptible to Brahmanical influence. The Mahayan School became a replica of Hindu ritualism. Nevertheless, Buddhist idealism retained its philosophical character as against the theological nature of the Brahmanical metaphysics. It never denied the existence of the world; it vaguely came near to the modern philosophical conception of the identity of the object and subject.

The preoccupation with the idea of "*Nirwana*" involved Buddhist philosophy into a maze of metaphysical speculations in which ground of pure fantasies the Brahmin scholastics not only held their own, but before long turned the table. Sankaracharya had no difficulty in proving that the entire system of the materialist-rationalist Buddhist philosophy was incompatible with the doctrine of "*Nirwana*". The priestly monopoly of ideology was reasserted after it had been shaken by the Buddhist Revolution.

The dynamic view of nature attained a high degree of clarity with Jains. The dialectic logic developed by the Jain philosophers was later on condemned by Sankaracharya as "an unsettling style of reasoning". It was, indeed, unsettling for the rigid orthodox logic which set up an imaginary absolute standard.. Once the absoluteness of the standard of truth is disputed, the whole airy structure of doctrines and dogmas, reared upon that foundation, necessarily collapses.

The Jain philosophers maintained that contradictory attributes, such as being and non-being, could belong to one and the same thing. They subjected the conceptions of absoluteness, unity and eternity to their "unsettling style of reasoning". The result was rejection of the doctrine of the Brahman. The disruptive effect of their views and methods of reasoning can be judged from the charge Sankaracharya brought against them: "If you maintain that the heavenly world and final release exist or do not exist, and are eternal or non-eternal, the absence of all determinate knowledge, which is implied in such statements, will result in nobody's acting for the purpose of gaining the heavenly world and final release."

The Jains also believed in Soul; but they conceived it as a constantly changing entity—something very different from the orthodox "simple and immortal" divine spark in man. They thought that soul was composed of an infinite number of particles—"soul-atoms"—which was constantly increasing and decreasing. That, in their opinion, did not affect the permanence of the soul; for, a thing can be permanent and non-permanent at the same time. For example, although the water is constantly flowing, the stream of water is always there. The ontological counter-part of this logic is obvious: The phenomenal world is permanent and real with all its continual changes and transitoriness.

In the antique period, as well as in the middle-ages, Indian society never quite reached a level of evolution where the power and position of the priesthood could be successfully disputed by a new social class which, by its very nature, would be the standard-bearer of scientific thought and thus lay down the foundation of philosophy.

The distinctive feature of Indian speculation, common to all schools, including even those materialist and quasi-materialist ones, some records of which have come down in history, is the anxiety to find release from the bondage of the life in this world. This morbid conception of life originated in the chaotic and depressing conditions resulting from the disintegration of the antique social order. The picture of social conditions towards the close of the Epic Era, as depicted in the Mahabharata, is anything but bright. Such conditions were sure to beget pessimism as well as revolt. Legends, recorded in the Mahabharata, testify to the rise of the forces of revolt which sometimes were too powerful for the weakened Kshattriya ruling class. But that was an elemental movement, rather actuated by despair than inspired by the ideal of a new social order.

Pessimism was the prevailing spirit. All the schools of Indian speculation bear the stamp. All look upon nature as a source of bondage; the freedom was not to be had by bursting the bondage, that is, by conquering nature, but by the easier imaginary way of running away from the "evil". The idea of conquering the external nature never entered Indian speculation. Therefore, it could not ever attain the level of real philosophy. Self-mortification is not the conquest of nature. It is to block all the ways of knowing external causes. It means plunging into the dark ocean of blissful ignorance.

Self-mortification, however, had no place in the primitive Vedic religion which, like all natural religions, was "materialistic" in the vulgar sense of the term. Pessimism, begotten in the chaotic and miserable conditions of the disintegration of the tribal society, was seized upon by the priestly ruling class as the opportunity for expounding the pernicious doctrine of renunciation and self-mortification which became such an effective weapon in the struggle for maintaining their dominating position. Life is full of miseries, because the desires of man can never be satisfied. Control the desires, you will be free from the evils of nature, and all misery will cease. Eternal bliss will be yours. The triumph of this "spiritualist" view of life reflected a tremendous social reaction which, in its turn, deeply affected speculative thought for a long time to come. Even revolutionary Buddhism could not fully live down that corrupting tradition of a previous social reaction, and was eventually vitiated by the poison. The triumph of the doctrine of self-mortification as the way out of the miseries of life represented the defeat of the forces of dissatisfaction with, and revolt against, the established order of things.

The discontent with things as they are is the condition for their change. The replacement of discontent by resignation, of revolt by indifference, means stagnation of social energy. All striving for material progress ceases, and ideological evolution is correspondingly affected. The triumph of the reactionary priesthood in the class struggle of remote antiquity determined the peculiar feature of Indian speculative thought. The triumph of reaction, in its turn, was possible because there had not yet arisen a class which could lead Indian society out of the crisis resulting from the downfall of the tribal social order. In course of time, the relation of classes changed. More or less disruptive schools of speculation flourished. But they all bore, in a greater or lesser degree, the distinctive stamp which signified a very slow process of social evolution, and the consequent continuation of sacerdotal supremacy.

The urges of life compel man to take up the endless struggle with nature. In course of this struggle, man penetrates deeper and deeper into the mysteries of the Universe, and progressively these mysteries cease to be mysterious. Primitive empiricism gives birth to philosophy; philosophy is the mother of science, and finally science enthrones the venerable mother as the "science of sciences". The taboo on the joy of life, the perverse prejudice against the natural urges of life, emasculates man. It holds him back from the mission, given to him by his very being. Consequently, it precludes a free spiritual evolution. Man creates science and philosophy. When the conditions of his social existence set limits to his human existence, his thoughts are naturally distorted. Indian speculation presents such a picture of distorted thought.

Therefore, the rationalist, materialist and naturalist teachings of Kanad, Kapila, Gautama, Mahabir, Charbak* and others were ultimately buried under the ruins of the Buddhist revolution. Brahmanical reaction, reasserting itself in the scholasticism of Sankaracharya, choked all spiritual progress so successfully that a renaissance of the liberating thought of antiquity was delayed until it was too late. The Hindu ruling classes were so exhausted by the delirium of having overwhelmed a mighty revolution, that the country became an easy prey to foreign invaders. General prostration and stagnation, on the other hand, precluded the rise of new social forces corresponding to those which rescued Europe from the darkness of the pious and spiritual middle-ages. India remained spiritual because, owing to historical reasons, she was deprived of the blessings of modern science. Her spiritualism is the badge of social backwardness which brought her people slavery, degradation and degeneration.

Whatever record exists about the various schools of philosophical thought in ancient India, bears testimony to the fact that dissatisfaction with the Vedic Natural Religion gave rise to speculations about the origin of the world, which inevitably developed tendencies to explain the world in physical terms. In India also, physics preceded metaphy-

* Charbak taught: Pleasure is the object of life. Real Pleasure can be had only in this life. It is a mistake to sacrifice this life with the hope of having pleasure in some other existence. It is like running after a mirage. Religion makes men miserable by persuading them to abandon pleasure. Thus idle and indolent are not able to do what is necessary to earn enjoyment and pleasure. Religious ceremonials are all swindles invented by these men. They have neither meaning nor use. The world is there for men to enjoy and be happy. Everything there is of necessity. The followers of Charbak denied Buddhist nihilism, and scoffed at the idea of Nirwana.

sics. Much of the really philosophical thought of ancient India has unfortunately been lost. But from the fragmentary evidence recorded, that forgotten chapter of the spiritual history of India can be reconstructed. As everywhere, originally, in India also philosophy was materialism. The materialistic outcome of the speculations of the rebels against the Vedic Natural Religion, contained in the three systems of philosophy proper, namely, Vaisheshik, Sankhya and Nyaya, provided the inspiration for the greatest event in the history of ancient India,—the Buddhist Revolution. The spiritual development of India during nearly a thousand years, beginning from the seventh century B.C., was very largely dominated by materialist and rationalist tendencies. It is highly doubtful whether the Vedanta system was formulated before the end of that Golden Age of Indian history. Internal evidence clearly proves the opposite case. The main purpose with which Vedantist pantheism was developed was to combat the materialist systems of Kanad and Kapila as well as the revolutionary doctrines of Buddhism and the unsettling logic of the Jains. That being the case, it is permissible to maintain that in ancient India, until the fall of Buddhism, philosophy was largely materialistic. Even as late as the fourth century A.D., in the period of triumphant Hindu restoration under the Gupta dynasty, the Chinese traveller Fa Hien found in India no less than "ninety-six heretical sects, all of whom admitted the reality of worldly phenomena."

Sankaracharya constructed his rigidly logical, but philosophically ambiguous system of monism for combating Buddhist idealism. But the real enemy he had to contend with was the materialist traditions of the pre-Buddhist philosophy. His works are full of long polemics against materialist and naturalist doctrines, so much so that the fragments, profusely quoted by him, can serve as a reliable foundation for reconstructing the latter.

The following can be recontsructed as the summary of the "atheism and materialism" that Sankaracharya combated, from fragmentary evidences contained in his own works.

Religious doctrines are all meaningless words. Their foundation is the idea of God whose very existence cannot be proved. The God is the Creator, but he has no origin. If it is admitted that there must be a Creator and ruler of the world, then, there arises the question: Who created the Creator? Whence did he come? The Creator is said to be without beginning and without end; without any limit. But, after all, he is a Creator, which implies a personality on his part. The God is, indeed, considered to be the Creator. But a person cannot be without beginning and end and other limits. If the God is limited, then, is it not possible that there may exist a power over and above him? The God is believed to be all-powerful and all-pervading. But these attributes of the God cease to be what they are believed to be, as soon as they are imagined by man. Thus, the essence of the God, the Creator, disappears. Then, it is taught that desire is the cause of creation. From this, it follows that God himself is not free from desire. Further, if the Universe is created by the Will of God, then, God himself must have the feeling of want; for, wish grows out of want. The feeling of want destroys omnipotence, omniscience, completeness and all other super-human attributes ascribed to the God.

What has come down to us as the most authoritative and representative Hindu philosophy, was the creation of Sankaracharya. He was the ideologist of the Brahmanical reaction and feudal society which were re-established on the ruins of the Buddhist revolution. But all Sankaracharya's efforts for liquidating the traditions of the really philosophical thoughts of ancient India were a failure. This very important fact of the spiritual history of India is not realised. Yet, it is obvious from a critical study of Sankaracharya's work. He failed to meet the materialists on their ground. He could not refute their arguments. He had to fall back on the authority of the Scriptures, the repudiation of which had been the starting point of all philosophical thought in ancient India. Of all the great ancient rationalists, Kapila alone had admitted scriptural testimony as evidence. But that was only a formal concession. While declaring that the existence of God could not be proved, because there was no evidence, Kapila does not take scriptural testimony into account. Even the Vedanta Sutras themselves do not accept the Scriptures as answering all the questions raised by those dissatisfied with the dogmas of natural religion. "Not having found the highest bliss in the Vedas, Sandilya studied the Sastras."* The latter contain primitive rationalism which rejects the childish faith of the Vedic religion.

* Bhagavata.

So highly developed and powerful were the materialist and naturalist schools combated by Sankaracharya, that, whenever he tried to refute their arguments logically, he was driven to take up an essentially materialistic position. His pantheistic monism is inverted materialism. The Mayavad is a shame-faced recognition of the reality of the external world. It is only by degenerating into a dogmatis system of theology, which tries to reconcile even the gods of the Vedic natural religion with the metaphysical conception of Brahman, that Sankaracharya's system apparently escapes the glorious fate common to all systems of consistent pantheism. The fate is to corroborate the materialist view from the opposite direction.

Sankaracharya begins his commentary of the Vedanta Sutras with the assumption, that it is a matter not requiring any proof that the object and the subject are opposed to each other as much as darkness and the light are, and therefore cannot be identical. Starting from this absolute dualistic conception, his monotheism could be established only by the absurd sophistry of the doctrine of Maya. In order to establish the "reality" of an existence, which is simply assumed, and which, by its very nature, as well as admittedly, cannot be proved, the perceptible and provable existence is declared to be an illusion. The Brahman is associated with a certain power called *Avidya* which is the cause of all the appearances of the world. This power cannot be called "Being", for Being is only Brahman. But immediately it is admitted that it cannot be called "non-being", for, at any rate, it produces the appearance of this world. It is in fact a principle of illusion: The undeniable cause, owing to which there seems to exist a material world. Maya thus constitutes the *Upadhana*, the material cause of the world. Maya belongs to the Brahman, as a *Sakti*. The material cause of the world is Brahman in so far as it is associated with Maya.

This doctrine obviously contradicts the conception of Brahman as a unitary and absolute existence. Brahman is destitute of all qualities. It is devoid of all attributes—thought, activity etc. Yet, Maya is assumed to be its *Sakti*. Moreover, Maya is conceived as an existence parallel to Brahman. The idea of "association" presupposes two entities; similarly, that of belonging. Since it is admitted that Brahman may be regarded as the material cause of the world, it cannot be an immaterial entity. Two qualitatively different things can never stand in relation of causality. On the other hand, if the position of Brahman is not compromised by placing it in a relation of causality with the material world, then, the latter must be granted an independent existence. Whatever may be its cause, the Brahman cannot be its origin. Sankaracharya gets out of this difficulty by falling back on religion. He argues: "If it be objected that on the Vedanta doctrine there is no room for a moving power, as in consequence of the oneness of Brahman no motion can take place, we reply such objections by pointing to the fact of the Lord being fictitiously connected with Maya." This sort of argument carries little conviction to those who do not start from the fundamental dogma of religion. To begin with, the material world is dismissed as an illusion. The "real" existence has nothing to do with it. Then, the question about the moving forces of the phenomenal world is answered by asserting dogmatically that the metaphysical entity Brahman becomes a personal God and maintains a fictitious connection for causing the phenomenal world. All these curious devices and grossly fallacious arguments were adopted to combat materialistic monism.

The unreality of the phenomenal world is the fundamental dogma of the Vedanta system. But in order to refute the idealistic school of Buddhism, Sankaracharya himself rejected the very dogma. The Buddhist idealists held that cognition was exclusively an internal process; not that it had no connection with the external object, but that it was self-contained; the external objects existed only in their relation to the mind. The substantial residue of objects is atoms, the rest being form; but the atom cannot be conceived by mind.

In combating this doctrine, Sankaracharya writes: "The non-existence of external things cannot be maintained, because we are conscious of external things. Why should we pay attention to a man who affirms that no such thing exists?" Why should we, then, take Sankaracharya seriously when he talks of Maya? He proceeds: "That the outward thing exists apart from consciousness, has necessarily to be accepted on the ground of the nature of consciousness itself. Nobody, when perceiving a post or a wall, is conscious of his perception only; but all men are conscious of posts and walls as objects of their perceptions. Even those who contest the existence of external things, bear witness to their existence when they say that, what is an internal object of cognition, appears like something external. No one says that Vishnumitra appears like the son of a barren mother. If we accept the truth as it is given to our consciousness, we must admit that the objects of perception appear to us as something external. Because, the distinction of thing and idea is given in consciousness; the invariable concomitance ot idea and thing has to be considered as proving only that the thing constitutes the means of ideas, not that the two are identical. It cannot be asserted in any way that the idea, apart from the thing, is the object of our consciousness; for, it is absurd to speak of a thing as the object of its own activity. The variety of mental impressions is caused altogether by the variety of external things perceived. This apparent world whose existence is guaranteed by all the means of knowledge, cannot be denied."

Here, Sankaracharya is combating his whole philosophy. Once the issues are joined on the philosophical ground, the triumph inevitably goes to materialism. When Sankaracharya himself had to expound the above purely materialistic theory of cognition, it is evident how powerful was the current of materialist thought which influenced the spiritual life of ancient India for nearly a thousand years, until the downfall of Buddhism.

The rise and fall of materialism in ancient India approximately coincided with the same events in Greece. The period of spiritual darkness following thereupon was brought to a close in Europe by the reassertion of materialist and rationalist thoughts on the strength of the achievements of modern science. That did not happen in India. Consequently, the spiritual heritage of India still remains to be rescued from her cultural ruins. What prevented India from following the same course of spiritual development as Europe, after having done that, up to only several hundred years ago, from the remotest days of human history?

In ancient Greece, philosophy was created by the class of merchant-princes, whose social position was antagonistic to the power and privilege of the priesthood. In ancient India, the trading class never attained such a position in society. Self-sufficient village economy prevented the growth of trade on a national scale. The small surplus product of the village artisan was exchanged in local markets. Practically, the entire surplus agricultural produce went for the payment of taxes. It is recorded that during the centuries immediately preceding the Christian era, commodities such as precious stones, spices and silk, were exported from southern India to Greece and Rome. But the maritime trade was carried on by the "Javans" (Greeks), who are reported to have crowded the markets of southern Indian ports, and even been employed as soldiers by the Dravidian kings. Later on, the carrying-trade on the same route passed on to the hand of the Arabs. Foreign trade over-land, developed after the foundation of the Bactrian Kingdom, also was mostly carried on by the "Javans". Some trade in large volume, however, appears to have grown in the south, which fact explains the establishment and persistence of Hinayan Buddhism (the original philosophical form) in those parts. In the Brahmanical society of the north, development of trade was discouraged. In the earlier Brahmanical laws—of Manu and Kautilya—the trader does not figure as one of the main social classes. In this connection, it will be instructive to cite what Havell discovers as the cause of the spiritual superiority of Indo-Aryan culture.

"They (Vedas) represent the culture of a race of warrior-poets and philosophers who despised the arts of commerce and lived mostly by agriculture, with one hand on the sword and the other on the plough. They built no temples, but worshipped nature-spirits with simple sacrificial rites....The Aegean, Babylonian and Dravidian cultures were essentially mercantile civilisations with a more limited spiritual outlook, though in the nature of things, they were more concerned with the happiness which lies in material possessions than in spiritual thoughts."*

When the more civilised Dravidians were subjugated by the pastoral Aryans, the latter imposed upon the former, social laws which checked the growth of the trading class, and consequently of free thought. As regards "the happiness of material possessions", the beef-eating and soma-drinking Vedic priests were not averse to it. But in order to maintain themselves in the position of power and privilege, they could not let the masses participate in that happiness. Hence the "spiritual superiority" of the Indo-Aryan culture. The concern for the happiness of material possessions, not in the vulgar sense as was the case with the Vedic Rishis, but in the wide

* "Aryan Rule in India."

sense of conquering the forces of nature for the benefit of humanity, is the impulse to philosophic thought. Since the "spiritually superior" Indo-Aryan culture of the Vedic era did not feel this concern, philosophy remained unknown until the rise of the more progressive class of traders could not be altogether checked by priestly domination.

Buddhism is usually interpreted as the revolt of the Kshattriyas against Brahmanism. To some extent, it was so; but the mercantile class also entered into the social background of the revolution. For example, according to Hiuen Tsang, the famous University at the great Nalanda Monastery was founded by the munificence "of five-hundred merchants who were disciples of Buddha." The merchants must have attained some social importance under the Buddhist kings. Upon the restoration of Brahmanism, under the Guptas, they were again subjected to economic limitations and social discriminations.

The codes of Manu, compiled in the fourth century A.D., placed the merchants under all sorts of disadvantages. It was from that time, that sea voyage came to be counted as one of the causes of "impurity". The missionary work of Asoka had promoted the habit of travelling over sea. Indian traders had been visiting the Malayan Islands and China. The result must have been a widening of vision which found its reflection in the Hinayan (philosophic) school of Buddhism which for a long time resisted Brahmanic reaction in southern India. Sea voyage was prohibited by Manu because it encouraged heretical views. In the absence of a mercantile class, as an independent and powerful social force, Indian speculative thought could not become philosophy, in the correct sense. And the absence itself was the product of the given social relations. Land was held by the Kshattriyas and the Brahmins, —classes which, by their very social being, were hostile to trade. In order to be so powerful as to dispute the ideological monopoly of the priesthood, the free-thinking merchants must grow out of the rich landed aristocracy. But in India, the latter was closely associated with the Brahmins. That relation was established in consequence of the ruinous civil war recorded in the Mahabharata. The Kshattriyas were so seriously weakened that they had to re-admit the supremacy of the Brahmins. This peculiar complex of social relations determined the specific form of Indian thought, and explains why materialism practically disappeared, after it had flourished so well in an earlier period.

# CHAPTER IV

## RATIONALISM, MATERIALISM AND IDEALISM

FOR the first ten centuries of the Christian era, Europe lay prostrate under the dismal ruins of the Roman Empire. Whatever economic and intellectual activity was there, was confined to the Church and the monasteries. In contrast to that condition in Europe, trade flourished in the Asiatic and African provinces of the fallen Empire. Those parts of the world had eventually come under the rule of the Arab Muslims who had extended their sway as far as Spain. In the tenth century, Andalusia was the market for all the treasures of the East. It was connected with the distant parts of the vast Muslim Empire with arteries of trade pulsating with the blood of a new life. That quickened intellectual activity rescued from the ruins of the Roman Empire the learning of ancient Greece. It was soon to become the inspiration for the modern civilisation.

The great result of Greek culture, as embodied in the works of Aristotle, was preserved mostly by the Arabs, together with the Jews, to be introduced in Europe not until the twelveth century. Before that time, Aristotle's logic alone had been taken over by Christian learning; but the philosophical and scientific teachings of Aristotle came to Europe through the intermediary of the Arab Muslims. They learned Aristotelian philosophy from the Alexandrian school; there they also learned the scientific doctrines of Hipparchos, Hypocrates, Euclid, Galen and others. Besides, Aristotelian metaphysics and science, Europe also learned scepticism—that solvent of faith—from the Arabs.

Owing to the mixture of Greek, Jewish, Egyptian, Assyrian and Persian culture, the Muslim world, in the earlier centuries of its history, was the seat of cosmopolitanism. So long as peoples live apart, they regard each other's religion as a mass of absurdities—heathenism, heterodoxy, etc. Closer contact breaks down the wall of ignorance. It stands to the credit of Arab philosophers to have conceived for the first time the idea of a "common divine origin" of all religions. They went even farther and made the bold suggestion that all religions represented efforts of human mind to solve the great mysteries of life and nature, and that the effort more reconcilable to reason was the greater and nobler and sublimer. This rationalistic idea of religion attained the highest degree of clarity with Averroes who, throughout the middle-ages, dominated the intellectual life of Europe.

The thirteenth century opens a new era. The revival of economic life—trade and industry—gave a new impetus to scientific thought. Europe, exhausted by the barbarism of the early middle-ages, turned to antique traditions for inspiration. But they were monopolised by the Church, and corrupted to suit its purpose. The new life, therefore, quickened the antagonism to Christian learning, and welcomed everything that reinforced it in the struggle. The Arabian philosophy came to its aid.

"There had been scepticism (in Europe) before

the thirteenth century, but no real incredulity; this doctrine and that doctrine had been disputed, rejected; but the foundation of Christian doctrine had never been touched. It was the foundation which was touched when the idea was reached that all religions have a common ground. This was in the thirteenth century, and may be traced to Arabian influence."*

Theological dogmas no longer satisfied human spirit, in the throes of a re-birth. The certainties of the rising scientific knowledge stood in glaring contrast to the absurdities of theological learning. One by one, the various dogmas of faith were invaded by positive knowledge. There began the process of a radical change in the conception of the world. The belief in super-natural agencies began to be shaken by an ever widening knowledge of the natural agencies. Dogmatism was challenged by rationalism. The articles of faith were questioned by reason. The supreme Divine Will, operating arbitrarily, defying all explanation, began to be replaced by invariable Natural Laws. This mighty change took place slowly, but the process was irresistible. Because, it reflected the operation of new social forces.

Doubt was let loose as the great solvent of theology. Reason still remained subservient to faith. But it began to assert itself. Metaphysics appeared as the fore-runner of modern science. The scholastic learning rose with the object of making a reconciliation between dogmas of religion and reason. That was as early as in the nineth century, when the founder of Scholasticism, Scotus Erigena, undertook

* Lewes, " The History of Philosophy ".

the justification of the dogmas of religion rationally. He taught: "Reason is first, in nature, and authority, in time. For, although nature was created together with time, authority did not begin to exist from the beginning of nature and time. But reason has arisen with nature and time from the beginning of things. Reason itself teaches this. For, authority no doubt hath proceeded from reason, but reason not by any means from authority. And all authority which is not approved by true reason turns out to be weak. But true reason, seeing that it stands firm and immutable, protected by its own virtues, needs not to be strengthened by any confirmation of authority."*

The standard of revolt was raised, though with circumspection. Cautiously, a place was secured for reason, from which it could open an attack upon faith. Once faith submits herself to explanation by reason, there is nothing to prevent the process from reaching the point where she must be rejected as incompatible with reason. The Church naturally thundered in indignation to scare the upstart. But the latter was called forth by the rise of new social forces which could not develop any farther without bursting the bonds of the dogmas and articles of faith. The Church had outlived her mission, and had become too narrow to contain the rising spirit of humanity. The standard of revolt, raised by Erigena, was held aloft and carried forward boldly by Rosellinus, Abelard and a whole host of others. The former was the first to attack the doctrine which had come to be known as "Realism". The Church had

* Maurice, "Mediaeval Philosophy."

adopted the Platonic doctrine that abstract notions constituted the real existence. Rosellinus declared that general terms were "mere names", and argued that there did not exist a thing called colour apart from coloured things. He boldly pushed his ideas and proclaimed that the Trinity of Christian theology was incompatible with unity of real existence. He was accused of heresy and died a martyr to the cause of progress. But the "Nominalist" school of Scholasticism, he founded, contributed largely to the triumph of rationalism.

So irresistible were the new forces that before long the more far-seeing among the orthodox churchmen preferred subterfuse to open attack against the enemy. The canonised Archibishop of Canterbury, Anselm, for example, "consecrated the previleges of Reason by showing the harmony between reason and faith." The result, however, was only to fan the flames of reason. Still for several centuries, reason remained more or less under the tutelage of faith; nevertheless, the authority of the latter was undermined, and the trail of spiritual freedom was blazed.

The great scholastic dispute between the "Realists" and "Nominalists" degenerated in a thick cloud of words. Reason again appeared to be overwhelmed by faith. Scepticism tended towards the blind-alley of mysticism. At that juncture, Roger Bacon rose as the fore-runner of the movement demanding greater freedom of thought and wider reach of enquiry. He also pleaded for the cultivation of mathematics and physics, and suggested rejection of the blind servility to scriptural text. Bacon was a pupil of the Arab philosophers and founders of systematic physical research. He lived in the latter half of the twelveth century.

Until then, rationalism had developed within the bounds of theology; now it threatened to burst the bounds. Europe still thought in terms of religion, and the Church was the patron of culture. Bacon considered the Scholastics of both the schools as barbarians in comparison to Aristotle and his Arab disciples. But he would not bow blindly even before his masters. He found a surer guide in experience. Though a monk, he devoted himself to the study of astronomy, mathematics and optics. He declared that mathematics and experiment were the only way to knowledge. He wrote:

"In every science, we must follow the best method, and that is to study each part in its due order, placing that first which is properly at the commencement, the easy before the difficult, the simple before the complex. And the exposition must be demonstration. This is impossible without experiment. We have three means of knowledge; authority, reason and experiment. Authority has no value unless its reason is shown; it does not teach, it only calls for assent. In reasoning, we commonly distinguish a sophism from a demonstration by verifying the conclusion through experiment. Experimental science is the mistress of speculative sciences."

Bacon found rationalism inadequate, and opened the way to empirical knowledge. He clearly grasped the idea that philosophy must be based on scientific knowledge. He ridiculed the attempt to solve physical questions by reason. Referring to the rationalists, he jestingly remarked: "If you ask of these doctors what is the cause of combustion, they can only answer that the cause is occult." The realisation of the inadequacy of scholastic rationalism prepared the ground for the reassertion of materialism.

In course of his famous controversy with Thomas Aquinas, the greatest of orthodox Christian theologists, the rationalist Don Scotus raised the momentous question: "Can matter think?" Then appeared Ockham in the beginning of the fourteenth century to liquidate Scholasticism. He was a freethinker and as such boldly separated the questions of philosophy from the questions of faith. He declared:

"In the question of Divine Intelligence being the first efficient cause of all that exists, as a philosopher, I know nothing about it, experience not instructing us in what way the cause of causes operates, and reason having neither the power nor the right to penetrate the divine sanctuary."

Ockham stands out as a pioneer of modern materialism by virtue of his famous maxim: "Don't multiply entities." Until then, the practice had been to invent a universal, generic or nomenal conception to account for any phenomenon. A multitude of such imaginary conceptions were attached to one single thing. For example, a Socrates could be understood by the notion of "Socrateity", humanity, animality, bipedity, so on and so forth. Naturally, there could be no understanding in such a maze of imaginary conceptions in which the only being really existing was simply drowned. The scholastics had disputed about reality either of the particular or of the universal. The rationalist "Nominalists" did not go to the extent of liberating themselves from the vicious circle of that duality. "Ockham's razor" cut the Gordian knot. He taught: Be satisfied with the real entity; don't multiply entities; start from the given concrete. The implication clearly is that there is nothing beyond the material world accessible to our understanding.

"The sixteenth century marks its place in history as the century of revolutions; it not only broke the chain which bound Europe to Rome, it also broke the chain which bound philosophy to Scholasticism and Aristotle. It set human reason free; it proclaimed the liberty of thought and action. In the vanguard of its army, we see men who must always excite our admiration and our gratitude for their cause and for their courage. They fell fighting for freedom of thought and utterance—the victims of a fanaticism, the more odious because it was not the rigour of belief, but of pretended belief. They fought in those days of the great struggle between science and prejudice, when Galileo was a heretic, and when the implacable severity of dogmatism baptised in blood every new thought born into the world."*

The deposition of Aristotle, the recognition of the inadequacy of the dogmas of faith, the worship of reason, however, could not as yet lead to the freedom from all authority. Even in the fifteenth century, Aristotelian logic remained the corner-stone of Christian theology. To contradict Aristotle was to disobey the Church. The position is illustrated by

* Lewes, "History of Philosophy".

the following story. A student, having discovered some spots in the sun, told a priest of his discovery. The priest remonstrated: "My son, I have read Aristotle many times, and I assure you there is nothing of the kind mentioned by him. Go, rest in peace; and be certain that the spots which you have seen are in your eyes, and not in the sun."

Giordano Bruno had the courage and conviction to contradict Aristotle. The latter had taught that the world was finite. Bruno declared that it was infinite and subject to an eternal and universal revolution. Aristotle believed the earth to be stationary. Bruno declared that it was in movement; that there were many worlds. He disputed the infallibility of the Church as regards science, holding that this earth of ours, on which the Church ruled, was not the central point of the Universe, it being one of an infinite number of worlds revolving in endless space. Deprecating the prevailing method of looking inside for the source of knowledge, he exhorted men to turn their eyes upon the nature. Though a Dominican monk, Bruno also was one of the early pioneers of modern materialism. He conceived of the identity of object and subject, of thought and being.

Bruno was burned as a heretic. But faith had lost its hold even on the minds of men who pretended to defend her sovereignty. "The Inquisition was vigilant and cruel, but among its very members, there were sceptics. Scepticism, with a polish of hypocrisy, was the general disease. It penetrated almost everywhere from the cloister to the Cardinal's palace."*

* Lewes, "History of Philosophy".

Old beliefs and traditional values having been thus shaken, the triumph of the Renaissance movement was inevitable. Europe opened the chapter of modern civilisation inspired with the desire to acquire scientific knowledge, and the inspiration was drawn from the materialist thought developed in ancient times.

Descartes liberated philosophy from the fetters of theology, with his new method which started from absolute doubt. The reign of authority was at an end. Nothing should be accepted as true until it was proved, and the standard of proof was not authority, but reason. He demanded that even theology should not be immune from reason. "I have always thought that the two questions of the existence of God and the nature of the soul were the chief of those which ought to be demonstrated rather by philosophy than by theology, for, although it is sufficient for the faithful to believe in God, and in that the soul does not perish with the body, it certainly does not seem possible ever to persuade the infidel to any religion, nor hardly to any moral virtue, unless we first prove to them these two things by natural reason."*

Once God and soul are placed under the stepmotherly care of philosophy with her iconoclastic method, nothing but dire misfortune can overtake those venerable prejudices. You can just as well take a fish out of water and let it thrive on the high and dry land. Disguised as an humble "faithful", the infidel threw down the fateful gauntlet to faith together with her shady entourage of teleology, theo-

* "Meditations".

logy and metaphysics, which had for ages served as so many fetters on the spirit of man. Starting with an absolute doubt about everything, the reality and veracity of which could not be established by sense-perception, Descartes rejected authority as testimony of truth. That logically led to the deposition of theology from the proud position it had occupied for more than a thousand years. Nothing should be accepted as true unless it was proved to be so, and the standard of truth was not authority, or the mystic fantasy called revelation, but reason.

Descartes expounded a mechanistic doctrine about the origin of the Universe. He started laying down the foundation of modern physics with the following declaration: "Although we know for certain that God created the world at once, it would be of eminent interest to see how the world might have evolved" by itself. The existence of God is assumed, quite unnecessarily, as the first cause of motion; but in the actual process of the evolution of the Universe, absolutely no place was left for the God. Together with elder çontemporary, Francis Bacon, Descartes most emphatically rejected the doctrine of the Final Cause. He said: "We can only presume it, since the God did not take us into his counsel. This habit of searching for a Final Cause has no use in physical and natural things." His theory of vortices explained the evolution of the Universe out of matter and motion. He tried to improve the ancient atomist theory by freeing it from the fallacy of action at a distance. He denied the existence of empty space on the ground that, the essence of substance being extension, wherever there is extension, there is substance; consequently, there can be no empty space. The substance which fills the space is assumed to be divided into angular particles. The mass of matter is in motion. The angular particles are ground into spherical forms. The smaller particles, rubbed off, constitute a second and more subtle kind of matter. The first goes into the constitution of luminous bodies, suns etc. There is still a third kind of matter, less fitted for motion. Out of these are formed the opaque bodies, earths, planets, etc. The second make the transparent substance of the sky. The motion takes the form of revolving circular currents—vortices. So, the coarse matter is collected to the centre of the vortex, while the second, finer matter, surrounds it, and by its centrifugal effort constitutes light. The planets are carried around the sun by the motion of the vortex.*

The Cartesian theory of vortices marks the beginning of modern physics and cosmology. In the beginning, the hypothesis appeared to be contradicted by the Newtonian physical theories which relied more on atomism in its original form. But modern physics vindicates the Cartesian hypothesis of an all-pervasive substance.

The credit for the definite inauguration of a new philosophy on the basis of experimental science and with the aid of inductive logic goes also to Francis Bacon. He started the enunciation of his "new method" with the following observations: "Through all these ages, the smallest part of human industry has been spent upon natural philosophy, though this ought to be esteemed as a great mother of all the

* Whewell, "Inductive Sciences".

sciences. Let none expect any great promotion of the sciences, unless natural philosophy be drawn out to particular sciences, and, again, unless particular sciences brought back to natural philosophy." Having criticised the "perverseness and insufficiency of the methods which have been pursued," he goes on: "Men have sought to make a world from their own conceptions. A sudden transition is made from sensible objects and particular facts to general propositions, which are accepted principles, and round which disputation and arguments continually revolve. The way that promises success is the reverse of this. It requires that we should generalise slowly, going from particular things to those that are but one step more general; from those to others of still greater extent, and so on to such as are Universals. By such means we may hope to arrive at principles, not vague and obscure, but luminous and well defined, such as Nature herself will not refuse to acknowledge. The evidence of sense, helped and guarded by a certain process of correction, I retain; but the mental operation which follows the act of sense, I, for the most part, reject; and instead of it, I open and lay out a new and certain path for the mind to proceed in, starting directly from the simple sensuous perceptions."

In its fight with religion and theology, rationalism had developed into materialism. Both Descartes and Bacon professed lip-loyalty to the idea of God. But in reality they laid down the foundation for modern materialism. Bacon enunciated the fundamental principles of a purely materialistic epistemology. As a matter of fact, he even tended to go a bit farther, when he refused to attach any value to "the mental operation". Evidently, he was fighting shy of the idea of soul. But in course of time, science revealed that mental operations also were determined by the laws of the physical world.

On the basis of the pioneering work accomplished by a number of great scientists, like Copernicus, Kepler, Galileo and others, Newton formulated the Law of Universal Gravitation, the verification of which by a series of observed facts definitely established the mechanistic view of nature. Newton expounded the "new philosophy" as the Natural Philosophy. For all practical purposes, it was materialism. And the Newtonian Natural Philosophy dominated the intellectual life of Europe until the successive achievements of science, inspired by it, contributed to the materialistic and rationalist thought, developed throughout the ages, into the comprehensive system of modern materialism.

Theology is developed, in course of spiritual development, when man begins to question about the nature of the creator whom he had previously manufactured out of his own imagination. The anthropomorphic God is gradually transformed into the metaphysical Supreme Being. That is the function of theology. Pantheism is the logical consequence of a consistent theology; and it leads directly to atheism. To prevent that catastrophic culmination of the religious mode of thought, speculative and idealistic philosophy steps in to confuse the logical line of development. Speculative philosophy is the attempt to explain the concrete realities of existence from the standpoint of a hypothetical Absolute. Objective truth is never reached that way. Failing to understand the world, speculative philosophy declares it a figment of our imagination. A search after truth, which begins from the concrete, reveals the eternalness of nature, having no place for a creator or a Supreme Being. Therefore, speculative philosophy avoids the simple and right course, and beats about the bush endlessly.

The "new philosophy" inaugurated by Descartes developed in two distinct directions, apart from the path of experimental science opened up by Newton and others. Of the two philosophical tendencies, one culminated in modern materialism, and the other developed in the contrary direction of idealism ("philosophical spiritualism"). The respective origins of the two antithetical lines of development are to be traced to the two great philosophers, Spinoza and Leibniz.

Spinoza brought theology to its logical conclusion. He expounded a mathematically rigorous system of pantheism with the inevitable implications of atheism and materialism. The cardinal principles of Spinoza's philosophy are: Unity of all that exists; regularity of all happenings; and the identity of matter and spirit. With these principles, Spinoza stood on the ground of materialism, although as a pantheist he conceived the substratum of the world as "soulful matter". Spinoza's philosophy therefore matured in three different directions: 1. In the poetry of Lessing, Herder and Goethe; 2. In the French Enlightenment of the eighteenth century; and 3. In the German classical philosophy of Schelling, Hegel and Feuerbach. Finally, Marx and

Engels gathered all the three threads to weave them into the system of dialectic historical materialism.

Spinoza's doctrine of "creation" was the ideology of a transition period. Rationalism had destroyed the Christian dogma—of creation out of nothing; at the same time, science was not yet developed enough to provide a purely materialistic explanation. Spinoza completely destroyed the old, and laid the foundation for the new. He condemned absolute ideas as abstractions arising from the infirmity of thought. He held that "transcendental ideas", thus formed, are necessarily obscure, inadequate, and therefore erroneous. Thought is the correlate of existence; mind is the obverse of matter, coextensive and co-intensive. All movement of matter is paralleled by the movement of mind, the external order is identical with the internal order. And whatever is conceived by intellect exists in the external world. In other words, ideas are but reflections of external things, having objective existence. Spinoza was a strict determinist. He argued: "Forging iron is only possible when we have a hammer; but to have the hammer, we must forge it, which presupposes another instrument, and so on *ad infinitum*. The materialist implication of this argument is made evident by Spinoza's famous axiom: "No two things can influence and affect each other, which have not some property in common."

This axiom completely destroys the dualist conceptions of matter and spirit. Should spirit influence and affect matter, as the condition for the creation of the phenomenal world, there must be some property common to both. If they affect each other, as they must do (otherwise there would be no creation), they are essentially the same. Consequently, in spite of its "soulfulness", Spinoza's substance is material. Spinoza's observations about the doctrine of the Final Cause are so very illuminating that they are better reproduced in his own words.

"Men do all things for the sake of an end, namely, the good or the useful they desire. Hence it comes that they always seek to know only the final causes of things. As within themselves and outside of themselves, they discover many means which are highly conducive to the pursuit of their own advantage, for example, eyes to see with, teeth to masticate with, vegetables and animals for food, the sun to give the light, the sea to nourish fish, etc.,—so they come to consider all natural things as means for their benefit; and because they are aware that these have been found, and not prepared by them, they have been led to believe that someone else has adapted these means to their use. For, after considering things in the light of means, they could not believe these things to have made themselves, but arguing from their own practice of preparing means for their use, they must conclude that there is some ruler or rulers of nature endowed with human freedom, who have provided all these things for them, and have made them all for the use of man. Moreover, since they have never heard anything of the mind of those rulers, they must necessarily judge of this mind also by their own; and hence they have argued that the gods direct all things for the advantage of man, in order that they may subdue him to themselves, and be held in highest honour by him. Hence, each has devised, according to his character, a different mode of worshipping God, in order that God might love him more than others, and might direct all nature to the advantage of his blind cupidity and insatiable avarice. Thus, this prejudice has converted itself into superstition, and has struck deep root into men's minds; and this has been the cause why men in general have eagerly striven to explain the Final Cause of all things. But while they sought to show that Nature does nothing in vain, they seem to me to have shown nothing else than that nature and the gods are as foolish as men. And observe to what a point this opinion has brought them. Together with the many useful things in nature, they necessarily found not a few injurious things, namely, tempests, earthquakes, diseases, etc. These, they supposed, happened because the gods were angry on account of offences committed against them by men, or because of faults incurred in their worship; and although experience every day protests, and shows by infinite examples that benefits and injuries happen indifferently to pious and ungodly persons, they therefore do not renounce their inveterate prejudice. For, it was easier to them to class these phenomena among other things, the cause of which was unknown to them, and thus retain their present and innate condition of ignorance, than to destroy all the fabric of their belief and excogitate a new one."

In a short compass, no more comprehensive and convincing criticism of the religious mode of thought could be given. Nevertheless, the roots of modern philosophical spiritualism also can be traced in the teachings of Spinoza. He built up a system on a set of definitions, axioms and propositions, conceived by "pure reason". The extreme clearness of these scaffoldings and the logical rigour of their application gave a mathematical precision to his system. Rationalism exhausted its possibilities. Supernatural authorities having been subverted, a new authority was enthroned in its place. That was Reason. Thus, the fundamental problem of philosophy was not yet solved. It only assumed a new, a more subtle form. How can the infallibility of reason be established? What is the sanction for this infallible standard? Whence do clear ideas come? Philosophy thus resolved itself into the question: "Have we, or have we not, any ideas antecedent to, and independent of, experience?" The answer in the affirmative led to modern idealism; that in the negative, to materialism.

Theology dominated learning much longer in Germany than in England and France. The influence of the materialistic thought of Gassendi, Descartes, Hobbes, Bacon, Locke and Newton, was stubbornly resisted in that country. Since the time of Descartes and Bacon, all great philosophers sought to construct a theory of the Universe independent of theology, with the aid of science. Efforts were also made to construct a modern system of metaphysics on the foundation of physical data. Those efforts were necessarily faulty, and handicapped with religious prejudices. Nevertheless, they irresistibly headed towards materialism, and by implication destroyed all faith: the dogmas and creeds of religion. The first great reaction to this movement began in Germany.. The great mathematician Leibniz was the leader of that movement. He constructed a scheme of the Universe from logical principles, accepted *a priori.* The "substance" of Descartes and Spinoza had provided the basis for a mechanical conception of the Universe. The essence of substance consisted in extension and thought. That was a conception pregnant with revolutionary potentialities. Leibniz opposed it with the conception of Force. Matter is the necessary consequence of force. Force is self-moved and immovable; self-divided, but not divisible. Matter evolves out of it. The dualism of matter and mind is overcome. Force is active and passive. In the latter state it is matter. Active force is the soul of matter—the impulse of its movement. Even these doctrines of Leibniz could not avoid a materialist conclusion.

Advance of science had forced theology to make determinism a part of its own system of dogmas. How to reconcile the conceptions of God and Soul with the idea of the mechanistic movement of nature? Leibniz undertook the impossible task. In order to strike materialism at the very root, he set about to reform the atomist conception. To prove that the Universe did not grow out of inanimate matter, he held that the atoms produced their own sensations; sensation is their innate quality. He held that the basic element of things are not atoms, but "monades". "In the place of material atoms appear intellectual individuals, in the place of physical, metaphysical points."*

Still, these "intellectual individuals" or "metaphysical points" are subject to a mechanistic law

* Zeller, "History of German Philosophy".

which is the postulated "pre-established harmony". Whatever may be the philosophical value of this postulate, it dispenses with the Creator. "The monades developed strictly necessarily, according to the forces inherent in them. None of them can, either in the sense of ordinary causality, or in that of pre-established harmony, be the productive cause of the rest. Even the pre-established harmony does not produce the monades, but only determines their condition, in precisely the same way as, in the system of materialism, the universal laws of motion determine the condition, that is, the relation in space, of the atoms."*

Everything in nature grows mechanistically—under a necessity, in an endless causal chain. It does not make any difference what name is given to the primary element. There is room neither for a Creator nor for a First Cause. As soon as the eternalness of the monades is assumed, there can no longer be any question of a Creator, no matter whatever may be the nature of the monades and their action. Leibniz's concern was to establish the First Cause of the phenomenal world, that is, the existence of an impersonal God. But the tragedy is that precisely that is dispensed with in his cosmology. The logical conclusion of the idea of the mechanical movement of nature is the endlessness of the causal series—both ways. Otherwise, backwards, the process must be traced to a Creator; and the mechanical movement immediately ceases to be mechanical as soon as that is done; it becomes teleological. The "pre-established harmony" is not the First Cause.

* Lange; "History of Materialism".

Newton postulated the *deus ex machina,* in order to go around the baffling problem of action at a distance. The problem did not exist in the system of Leibniz. His monades move, combine and react upon each other according to force inherent in themselves. Thus the "pre-established harmony" is only the principle of universal mechanism, metaphysically conceived. It does not exist apart from or independent of, the monades. It is their inherent quality. Thus, Leibniz, in spite of himself, arrives at the unity of matter and spirit, identity of thought and being. Here he lands on the ground of materialism. There can be no theism without dualism; religion is gone.

How would it look, should one regard the "pre-established harmony" as the First Cause? Simply, there would arise the question: "What is the cause of the First Cause? This question cannot be avoided, unless causality is abandoned. That would be against the whole system of Leibniz which rests upon the mechanism of causality. Whenever the causal chain breaks, it becomes inevitable to postulate a Creator, and determinism is gone. That is the irreconcilable contradiction between philosophy and theology. Instead of calling the "pre-established harmony" the First Cause, and thereby discard his whole philosophy, Leibniz, like all rationalist theologians, arbitrarily breaks off the causal series, and postulates an impersonal Creator. This irrationalism of the "rationalists" is forced; because, otherwise they would be driven to what may be called "inductive pantheism", if the term materialism is to be avoided. By following the causal chain, one must reach the point where dualism disappears, the line between spirit and matter vanishes, the identity of thought and being is established, and there remains nothing but a die-hard prejudice against materialism.

Leibniz introduced God in his godless philosophical system with the curious doctrine of the choice of the best world out of the infinite number of them possible to grow out of the mechanical movements and combination of monades. Everything goes on mechanistically, but an unseen hand guarantees that it goes in the right way. But, again, unless determinism of philosophy is secretly offered at the altar of theological dogma, the God appears to be a useless postulate, because the "pre-established harmony" should work out disregarding all outside interference. In the philosophy of Leibniz, "everything ends in bare, naked, matter of fact; the dependence of things upon God is an empty shadow. We may conceive the eternal essence of things, in whose nature God can alter nothing, just as well as eternal forces, by whose actual interaction is attained that reciprocal constraint which Leibniz brings about by the choice of God."*

The same author shows that the God of Leibniz cannot suck anything out of his thumb; that he does not create anything whatsoever. In whatever imaginary function earmarked for him, he has to do strictly with given facts,—the monades, existing eternally and moved mechanically by the force innate in themselves. The God "may be omnipotent,

* Baumann, "The Doctrines of Space, Time and Mathematics".

omniscient and anything else, but he cannot go beyond the essence of possibilities of the monades that exist independently of him and are conditioned by a pre-established harmony." The best that can be said of such a God is that he is a skilful mathematician and correctly appreciates the laws of mechanics which, however, he cannot change. The world will not be in the least affected for disregarding such a God who has no conceivable relation with it.

The greatest achievement of Leibniz is supposed to be the re-establishment of the "immateriality and simplicity of the soul". In this also, he contributed to the development of materialism, of course, unwillingly. The logical consequence of his doctrine of innate ideas is the admission of the identity of thought and being. The soul was saved at the cost of religion. For, religion disappears with the abolition of the separate existence of matter and spirit. And in the absence of religion, the soul ceases to be something super-natural. For fighting materialism, Leibniz was compelled to adopt a method which only defeated his end.

The monades are conceived as souls in embryo; but, on the one hand, they are not "divine sparks", because they are themselves eternal, existing by themselves, subject necessarily to forces inherent in themselves; on the other hand, they constitute everything—organic, inorganic, animal, human, etc. The doctrine of monades thus abolishes the qualitative difference between man and the lower animals, indeed, even the inanimate things. Thus, Leibniz unconsciously tended towards the theory of evolution formulated later by Lamarck and Darwin. The advance towards the recognition of a continuous connecting link between the lower and higher animals was unavoidable. The declaration was forced that animals possess souls as immortal as those of men. Pursuing the thoughts of Leibniz, one of his pupils came to the very significant conclusion that not only all animals had souls, but that their souls went through various stages and finally reached the degree of spirit, that is, human soul.

That was a position not very far from Darwin, but very very far from what Leibniz is supposed to have established—the "simplicity and immateriality of the soul". Human soul cannot be so simple if it results from a long process of evolution through successive animal stages. Nor is it immaterial, since it is changed through its contact with varying material objects. Materialism was the spontaneous expression of human spirit. Its march could be retarded, but not checked. Even in Germany, it asserted itself as evidenced by the failure of Leibniz to combat it. As a matter of fact, whoever tried to think philosophically, and to construct a system of philosophical thought, contributed to the development of materialism.

"One circumstance that helped to bring about so thorough a reform of philosophy was above all the defeat that materialism had inflicted upon old metaphysics. In spite of all refutation on special points, materialism lived on, and gained ground all the more, perhaps because it was not a narrow and exclusive system. Materialistic mode of thought very quietly gained ground in the positive sciences. The truth was that all the scholastic philosophy of the time could supply no sufficient counter-poise to materialism."*

Modern philosophy developed clearly and directly in the materialist direction in England. Hobbes was the founder of English materialism. Even before Newton, he rejected consciousness or innate idea as the standard of knowledge. He held that the origin of knowledge was to be sought outwards. The outside world is not to be explained by logic, but through the knowledge of its objective nature. About thought, Hobbes wrote: "Singly they are everyone a representation of appearance of some quality or other accident of a body without us, which is commonly called an object. Which object worketh on the eyes, ears and other parts of a man's body, and by diversity of working produceth diverity of appearance. The original of them all is that which we call sense, for there is no conception in a man's mind which hath not at first, totally or by parts, been begotten upon the organ of senses. The rest are derived from the original."

Hobbes further wrote: "Whatever we imagine is finite. Therefore, there is no idea, no conception of anything we can call infinite. No man can have in his mind an image of infinite magnitude; no man can conceive infinite swiftness, infinite time or infinite power. When we may say that anything is infinite, we signify only that we are not able to conceive the ends and bounds of the thing named, having no conception of the thing, but of our own inability. And therefore the name of God is used not to make

* Lange, "History of Materialism".
† "Leviathan".

us conceive him, for he is incomprehensible, and his greatness and power inconceivable, but that we may honour him. Also because whatsoever we conceive has been perceived first by the senses, either all at once, or by parts, a man can have no thought representing anything not subject to sense."*

In the light of this reasoning, religion turns out to be a mere glorification of the limitedness of human knowledge. The qualities attributed to God are mere words. They do not represent any objective reality, as far as man is concerned. Hobbes does not expressly deny the supersensual. But he places it beyond the ken of probability.

The Sensationalist school of philosophy, heralded by Hobbes, was founded by Locke. He proposed "to enquire into the original, certainty and extent of human knowledge." The substance of Locke's teaching is: Know the limits of your understanding; beyond these limits, it is madness to attempt to penetrate; within those limits, it is folly to let in darkness and mystery, to be incessantly wondering and always assuming that matters cannot be so plain as they appear, and that something lying deeper courts our attention. Locke clearly rejected the super-sensual as mere assumption. "Men extending their enquiries beyond their capacity, and letting their thought wander into those depths where they can find no sure footing, it is no wonder that they raise questions and multiply disputes which, never coming to any clear resolution, are proper only to continue and increase their doubts, and to

* "Human Nature".

confirm them at last in perfect scepticism."*

The semi-materialist Sensationalism was the outcome of rationalism. Reason could not claim to be the source of absolute knowledge without restoring the god whom it wanted to depose. Its pretensions were curbed by Sensationalism. There is a limit to human knowledge. Beyond the limit, there may be anything. Hobbes as well as Locke were the ideologists of the English bourgeoisie which had just made a compromise with the monarchy and feudalism. They proposed a division of labour with the Church. Religion and God could be left alone if they would give up interfering with things temporal. Sensationalism was not a system of philosophy. It was epistemology, and in that sense, it was frankly materialistic. Its fundamental principle was that sense perceptions were the only source of knowledge, and the senses perceived things which really existed outside. The English atmosphere of social compromise, in which the Sensationalist school flourished, did not permit it to develop its materialist principles fully and clearly. That was done in France as the ideology of the Great Revolution. The Sensationalist philosophy of Hobbes and Locke provided the point of departure for the great French materialists of the eighteenth century.

"Although modern materialism appeared as a system first in France, yet England was the classic land of the materialistic mode of thought. Here, the ground had already been prepared by Roger Bacon and Occam; Bacon of Verulam, who lacked almost nothing but a little more consistency and

* "Human Understanding".

clearness in order to be a materialist, was wholly a man of his age and nation, and Hobbes, the most consequent of modern materialists, is at least as much indebted to English tradition as to the example and precedence of Gassendi. It is true, indeed, that by Newton and Boyle, the material world-machine was again provided with a spiritual constructor; but the mechanical and materialistic theory of nature only rooted itself the more firmly, the more one could pacify religion by appealing to the Divine Inventor of the great machine."*

The Sensationalist philosophy of Locke, improved and amplified by Condillac, influenced the thought of eighteenth century Europe; it became the ideological basis of the bourgeois revolution. The object of Condillac's system was "to show how all our knowledge and all our faculties are derived from sensations." It is evident how he went farther than Locke. Rejecting reflection as a source of knowledge, Condillac traces the root of all knowledge to a single source—sensation. In doing so, he also broke with the Cartesian doctrine of innate ideas. Condillac was the first to disassociate mind from the metaphysical idea of soul, and conceive it as an integral part of the body. He holds that mind is nothing but a faculty out of which all the faculties evolve through the action of external objects on the senses. While praising Locke as the only philosopher who, after Aristotle, had written something worthy of notice on the question of cognition. Condillac criticised him: "The Englishman has certainly thrown great light on the subject. But he has left

* Lange, "History of Materialism".

some obscurity. All the faculties of the soul appear to him to be innate qualities, and he never suspected that they might be derived from sensation itself."

In addition to rejecting the doctrine that faculties are innate, the father of French materialism identified knowledge with sensation. But in his time, biological knowledge was as yet too backward to establish this experimentally. He maintained that inferences drawn from the examination of animal organisms were applicable to the observation of human mind. But comparative anatomy and physiology were still very backward. Then, the prejudices about soul forbade any such comparison in the sphere of psychology. "If men formerly thought they could understand man's body by dissecting it, and did not need the light thrown thereon by the dissection of animals, they were still less likely to seek psychical illustration in animals, denying as they did that animals also had mind."*

Nevertheless, Condillac suggested that psychological investigation, that is, enquiry regarding the nature and function of soul and mind, should be conducted not on the plane of metaphysical speculation, but as a branch of physiology. The English physician Hartley worked upon that suggestion. The impetus to his enquiry also came from Newton's suggestion that the cause of sensation was vibrations of ether. Hartley made the first attempt to explain psychological phenomena as actions of the physiological mechanism. Postulating that man consists of two parts, body and mind, Hartley tried to find the relation between the two, and came to the conclusion

* Lewes, "History of Philosophy".

that mental phenomena were produced by the vibrations of ether caused by external objects. Tracing the cause of all mental activities to etherial vibrations, Hartley destroyed the dogma of the immateriality of soul, and showed that mind was not a spiritual entity independent of, and antecedent to, the material body.

Erasmus Darwin, a name little known in the history of thought, approached the problem even more boldly than Hartley. He defined idea as "a contraction or motion, or configuration, of the fibres which constitute the immediate organ of senses", and held idea to be synonimous with "sensual motion in contra-distinction to muscular motion."* He not only challenged metaphysical speculations, but confronted the half-hearted Sensationalists with very pertinent questions. "If our recollection or imagination be not a repetition of animal movements, I ask, what is it? You tell me it consists of images or pictures of things. Where is this extensive canvass hung up? Or, where the numerous receptacles in which these are deposited? Or, to what else in the animal system have they any similitude? That pleasing picture of objects, represented in miniature on the retina of the eye, seems to have given rise to this illusive oratory! It was forgot that this representation belongs rather to the laws of light than to those of life; and may with equal elegance be seen in the camera obscura as in the eye; and that the picture vanishes for ever when the object is withdrawn."

Even the Sensationalists could not get rid of the

* Erasmus Darwin, "The Laws of Organic Life".

traditional belief that there is some sort of a spiritual entity in man which receives the impressions of the external objects. Erasmus Darwin not only exposed the groundlessness of that belief, but made an attempt to clear away the doctrine of image which had confused the theory of cognition, feeding idealism, on the one hand, and promoting scepticism, on the other. The logical conclusion of the views of Hartley and Erasmus Darwin was that ideas were produced in a long complicated physiological process, caused in the nervous mechanism by external objects.

The credit of founding the materialist theory of cognition belongs to the French scientist Cabanis. A disciple of Condillac, he detected the shortcoming of the master, indeed, of the entire Sensationalist school, which suffered from a serious weakness owing to the failure to take transmitted (through heredity) and previously stored impressions (instincts) into account. Owing to that defect, the Sensationalist explanation that mental phenomena were properties of the vital organism failed to carry conviction. The word "sensation" having a limited connotation—of immediateness and directness—even Condillac could not cure the basic defect of his materialism. It was for Cabanis to do so, who liquidated Sensationalism in favour of full-fledged materialism. He added "connate instincts" to direct and immediate sensations, as the source of mental phenomena. He thought it necessary to ascertain what was sensibility. He opens his enquiry with the question: "Does it always pre-suppose consciousness and distinct perception? And must we refer to some other property of living body all those unperceived impressions and movements in which volition has no part?" The enquiry, thus begun, led him to the following conclusion.

"Subject to the action of external bodies, man finds in the impressions these bodies make on his organs, at once his knowledge and the cause of his continued existence; for, to live is to feel; and in that admirable chain of phenomena, which constitute his existence, every want depends upon the development of some faculty; every faculty, by its very development, satisfies some want, and the faculties grow by exercise as the wants extend with the faculty of satisfying them. By the continual action of external bodies on the senses of man, results the most remarkable part of his existence."*

Here, the revolutionary principles of Sensationalism are freed from all limitations. This statement of those principles connects intelligence, desire, knowledge, etc. with the origin of vital movements. It abolishes the invidious distinction between life and mind. It makes mind a function of the living body. The mediaeval religious philosophy had subordinated mind to the soul which was placed above and beyond all material and physical conditions. In their revolt against theological domination, the philosophers of the Renaissance conceived mind as an independent entity. Descartes and Bacon adopted the doctrine. Since then, philosophy, particularly the semi-materialist Cartesian school, combated all suggestions which denied to intellect and reason a super-material character. To recognise the

* "The Relation between the Body and the Moral of Man".

independence of mind came to be regarded as the first principle of materialist philosophy. "To doubt this truth, was to overthrow all morality, to reduce man to the level of brute, to make religion a mockery. To doubt this truth, was in fact to incur the most incriminating charges of—materialism."*

Thus rationalism came to the aid of religion whose foundation it has previously sought to undermine by asserting the freedom of mind; metaphysical philosophy made peace with theology which it wished to abolish. But the process of ideological evolution, set in motion by changes in social conditions, and the necessity of constant progress, could not be arrested by such reaction. Philosophy could not be freed from metaphysical prejudices and the terror of being called materialist, unless and until mind was clearly demonstrated as a function of animal organism, developing simultaneously with it. That was not possible to be accomplished by speculation, however bold, or logic, however acute. The development of biology was the condition for it. The merit of Cabanis was to indicate the way in that direction. Unless mind was divested of all spiritual properties, and recognised as a function of the animal organism, no science of human knowledge could be possible. Sensationalism brought philosophy to that parting of ways. There were three ways ahead: Materialism, Scepticism and Idealism. Power of prejudice and objective difficulties still blocked the first; the second was visibly a blind-alley; so, the main current of thought followed in the third, to culminate in the classical German philosophy which,

* Lewes, "History of Philosophy".

however, was overcome by its own grandeur.

The Newtonian Natural Philosophy was introduced into France, then in the throes of a gigantic revolution, because it was considered to be less injurious to faith than Cartesianism. But in the hands of the disciples of Condillac, who subsequently came to dominate the intellectual life of Europe as the great Encyclopedists, the pious philosophy of Newton only promoted the cause of atheism and materialism. "For the complete working out of the cosmology founded by Newton, no more favourable circumstances, no more favourable tone of thought, could be found than those in France in the eighteenth century. The magnificent phenomena of the seventeenth century were renewed in increased splendour, and to the age of a Pascal and Fermat succeeded with Maupertuis and D'Alembert. the long series of French mathematicians of the eighteenth century, until Laplace, drew the last consequences of the Newtonian cosmology in discarding even the hypothesis of a Creator."*

The French materialism of the eighteenth century is elaborately developed in the monumental book "The System of Nature" which, though appearing as the work of Holbach, was in reality the collective production of a number of intellectual giants, such as Diderot, Buffon, De Tracy, Helvetius, and others. The book came to be known as the "Bible of Materialism" or the "Bible of Atheism". The book proposes to answer the question how to secure the happiness of mankind. The answer is summarised in the preface:

* Lange, "History of Materialism".

"Man is unhappy merely because he misunderstands nature. His mind is so infected by prejudices that one must almost believe him to be for ever doomed to error; the chains of illusion, in which he is so entangled from childhood, have so grown upon him, that he can only with the utmost trouble be again set free from them. Man disdained the study of nature to pursue after phantoms that dazzled him and drew him from the plain path of truth, away from which he cannot attain happiness. It is, therefore, time to seek in nature remedies against the evils into which fanaticism has plunged us. There is but one truth, and it can never harm us. To error are due the grievous fetters by which tyrants and priests everywhere succeed in enchaining the nations. From error arose the bondage to which nations are subject; from error, the terrors of religion, which brought about that men mouldered in fear, or fanatically throttled each other for chimeras. From error arose deep-rooted hatred and cruel persecutions; the continual bloodshed and the horrid tragedies of which earth must be made the theatre to serve the interests of heaven. Let us try, therefore, to banish the mists of prejudice, and to inspire man with courage and respect for his reason. If there is any one who cannot dispense with these delusions, let him at least allow others to form their own ideas in their own way, and let him be convinced that, for the inhabitants of earth, the important thing is to be just, benevolent, and peaceful."

There is a classical record of the ideals and sentiments of avowed materialists. This was written nearly two hundred years ago. Since then, the development of science has consolidated the foundation of materialism, having removed the logical weaknesses of its structure. But the high moral ideals of materialism, declared two hundred years ago, still remain the same even to-day. Therefore, all the attacks against materialism, made ostensibly in the name of justice, peace, goodness and morality, are palpably mistaken or purposely malicious.

The following are the fundamental principles of materialism as stated elaborately by the great French philosophers of the eighteenth century: Nature is the great whole of which man is a part, and by which he is influenced. Super-natural beings have always been creatures of imagination. There does not, and can not, exist anything beyond the sphere that includes all creatures. Man is a physical being, and his moral existence is only a special aspect of his physical nature, a particular mode of action, due to his peculiar organisation. The world shows us everywhere nothing but matter and motion. It is an endless chain of causes and effects; the most various elements are continually reacting on each other, and their different qualities and combinations constitute for us the nature of individual things. The nature of a thing is the sum of its properties and modes of action.

No more need be added to this exposition of materialism, on the level attained in the middle of the eighteenth century, than one or two characteristic quotations from the more prominent French Encyclopedists.

"Moral doctrines are frivolous, unless they are given practical shape in politics and legislation. Men are neither good nor bad by birth; they are ready to be one or the other in accordance as common interest unites or separates them. Great reforms can be introduced only when the stupid glorification of old laws and customs is combated; that is to say, ignorance is abolished." (Helvetius).

"A man without passion or wish would cease to be human. A man to whom everything is the same, who is deprived of all passions, who is self-sufficing, would no longer be a social being." (Holbach).

It is to fight this philosophy of the spiritual liberation of man, that modern idealism developed as the official philosophy of the post-revolutionary modern Europe.

Idealism places spirit before matter, thought before being, mind before body. It is the antithesis of materialism. Ideas as abstract categories, existing by themselves, independent of body, as spiritual forms or patterns for material phenomena, were first created by the poetic imagination of Plato. The imagination of the Sage of Athens conforms nicely with the super-natural doctrine of creation, common to all religions: A Divine Will, an Immaterial Force, or a Super-Natural Being created the phenomenal world out of nothing, or expressed itself as such. The essence of the conception is that an immaterial consciousness is prior to material being; in other words, thought not only precedes being, but is independent of it. Indeed, the material being is the product of, and governed by, an immaterial spirit. Since the immaterial cannot conceivably be comprehensible to the material, the world of spirit—the

First Principle of the Final Cause of the world—must always remain beyond the reach of human mind, whose operation is limited by sense-perceptions. Yet, the object of life is to penetrate into that forbidden paradise! Thus, life is split up into two distinct compartments, one governed by the inscrutable force of the other, but never able to comprehend the operation of that imperious category. How, then, can the unattainable object of life be reached? Through Faith. How can the impossible be possible? Through magic. Since perceptions are not reliable, there must be some divine inspiration. Scientific knowledge is set at discount; premium is placed upon "religious experience". These, in brief, are the main premises and logical consequences of the idealist philosophy; and from these, its close kinship, indeed identity, with religious spiritualism is evident.

The most orthodox exponent of modern Idealism was Bishop Berkeley. His mission was to combat materialism which developed powerfully during the seventeenth and eighteenth centuries. He re-established the old religion, in an apparently rationalised form, after it had been rudely shaken by the great rationalist and materialist thinkers of the seventeenth century. Berkeley defined his philosophy as follows: "I assert as well as you (materialists) that, since we are affected from without, we must allow powers to be without, in a being distinct from ourselves. But then we differ as to the kind of this powerful being. I will have it to be spirit, you, matter."*

---

* "The Dialogue between Hylas and Philomenes".

The editor of Berkeley's works writes: "This is the gist of the whole question. According to the materialists, sensible phenomena are due to material substance; according to Berkeley, to Rational Will."*

The militant Bishop did not mince words about the nature of the Rational Will. For him, it was not a metaphysical abstraction; nor was it an indefinable mystic force. He went boldly to honest anthropomorphism: It was the "Will of God". Apart from his frankly professed religious zeal, Berkeley had another axe to grind. It was, to save his philosophy from solipsism—the insane position that nothing exists but myself,—a position to which his epistemological doctrine logically led. Therefore, he hastened to qualify the disastrous doctrine by saying that the world is not my idea. Ideas are of divine origin. They are created in the human mind by the operation of the laws of nature which are determined by a spiritual cause. Thus, on the evidence of its most orthodox, authoritative and consistent exponent, idealist philosophy, in the last analysis, is religion. It can stand only on the hoary foundation of faith, be it clearly visible, or cleverly concealed. Therefore, on a rigorously philosophical ground, it cannot hold its own against materialism which relies upon verifiable scientific knowledge.

What Berkeley combated, to some extent successfully, was not materialism, but sensationalism. And even then, the issues he joined were not philosophical, but episte-

* A. C. Fraser. Introduction to the Oxford Edition of the Works of Barkeley ".

mological. He did not deny that senses received impressions from outside, but maintained that mind had nothing more than its own perceptions. All questions regarding the nature of the external world from which the impressions came, he dismissed as idle metaphysics. But whenever he was pinned down to that fundamental question of philosophy proper, he was compelled to admit that there must be a substance from which the external world is made, but asserted dogmatically, that the substance was not material, but spiritual. Consistently followed up, on the philosophical plane, Berkeley's philosophy must end in the position that there exists nothing. That would be giving a handle to scepticism, which he also wanted to fight. Therefore, he admitted the existence of the external world and could avoid defeat at the hands of materialism only by reviving religion, that is to say, by abandoning the ground of philosophy.

The materialism of the great philosophers of the seventeenth century (Bacon, Hobbes, Locke etc.), combatted by Berkeley, the most consistent exponent of modern idealism, had not defined the position so clearly as was subsequently done in the middle of the nineteenth century on the evidence of the epoch-making discoveries of the natural sciences. Yet, Berkeley measured up the potential strength of the enemy with a remarkable insight. His greatness as a philosopher consisted in his ability to grasp the revolutionary implications of Sensationalism more clearly than its founders themselves. The logical deduction to be made from the Sensationalist theory of cognition, a deduction not fully made by the propounders of the theory, is that consciousness has no existence *per se*; it is but a complex of sensations, created by external objects upon living matter, adequately organised. The primacy of being, established by this deduction, links up epistemology directly with the old physical hypothesis of Democritos and Epicuros.

Epistemological problems are not problems of metaphysics. They can be properly stated and satisfactorily solved only in the light of a mechanistic-physical, as against metaphysico-teleological, view of the Universe. The primacy of being admitted, the next necessary step is to reduce it to a common denominator,—matter; and the conception of matter itself runs the risk of being transformed into a metaphysical category, as for example, Spinoza's "Substance", unless it is expressed in material terms, that is, in terms of physics, mechanics and mathematics. Ultimately, philosophy came triumphantly out of the spiritual confusion of the middle-ages, to stand firmly on the foundation of the ancient materialism of Democritos and Epicuros. It was on the basis of atomism, revised by himself, that Descartes rested his mechanistic cosmology, thereby giving birth to modern philosophy as well as physics.

When Berkeley combated materialism as "the repugnant source of atheism and irreligion", it was still in an embryonic form, still to be demonstrated by the development of natural sciences. The position of philosophy in his time was as follows:

Our senses inform us of some sensible qualities, such as extension, colour, solidity etc. But logic teaches that these qualities must be the qualities of something; they cannot exist as abstract extension, colour or solidity, as taught by Plato. There must be something extended, coloured, solid, etc. What is that something? The answer to this question cannot be given speculatively. By raising this question, philosophy prepared the ground for the natural sciences. Mere contemplation of nature was no longer adequate for the extension of human knowledge. The objects themselves should be subjected to examination. But at the time of Berkeley, sciences were not yet able to answer conclusively the question raised by philosophy. Philosophers, who had broken away from theology and were searching for a physical and rational explanation of the world, generally admitted that there was a substratum of all the perceptible qualities. They called it the substance. But they pleaded ignorance about its nature, because it was beyond human comprehension. Nevertheless, they were forced to admit the existence of a material substratum as a support for all the qualities which could be comprehended. All the sensible qualities were inherent in the substance. The necessity for some synthesis of the attributes led to the inference of the existence of matter.

The fallacy and weakness of that position of contemporary philosophy enabled Berkeley to make the synthesis a mental one, and thus get rid of matter. The backwardness of the science of psychology and consequently of the theory of cognition made Berkeley's idealism possible. But as soon as the discoveries of natural science destroyed all doubt regarding the objective existence of things outside, and physiology demonstrated how these things are perceived by our senses, idealism was compelled to shift its ground; it gave up the common-sense view of Berkeley, and plunged into the fever-fantasies of Hegel and the pantheism of Schelling, thereby liquidating philosophy as such.

Even Berkeley himself could hold his ground against materialism only by abandoning philosophy in favour of anthropomorphic religion. Until his time, metaphysics had maintained that ideas were the appearances of things. Only the appearances are immediately known. As a practical man, Berkeley did not deny the existence of things immediately perceived, but maintained that they were nothing more than reflexions of the ideas of the perceiver. Hence his famous thesis "esse est percipe" (existence is to be perceived). He argued that appearances immediately known to us are the only reality. They are not appearances, but the real things. Only ideas are immediately known to us. Therefore, only ideas are things. By this argument, he tried to go around the question regarding the substance behind the appearances. Moreover, as regards the source of the sense-perceptions, he fell back upon the good old idea of God. God has endowed our mind with the faculty of having perceptions—ideas—out of nothing. The substance is spiritual.

Berkeley's boundless idealism, which outraged common-sense, rose as a reaction against scepticism inherent in the Sensationalist philosophy of Hobbes and Locke, and also against the materialistic implications of the teachings of the fathers of modern idealism—Descartes and Spinoza. These latter had constructed their universal systems on the foundation of the concept of "substance" which provided a sound basis for materialism. In view of the dangers, inherent in Cartesian metaphysics, the pantheism of Spinoza and even the new theology of Leibniz, Berkeley expounded what could be called "pure idealism" by rejecting the concept of substance in favour of a known cause. He denied the existence of matter as the substratum of sensible qualities, which, according to Locke, was a necessary inference from the knowledge of qualities. While proclaiming the existence of a material substratum, Locke had nevertheless declared it to be unknowable. Berkeley seized upon that sceptic element in Locke's philosophy. He contended that only the sense-perceptions are given to us. Anything beyond it, is pure metaphysics. He rejected the "unknown" substance as the phantom of the "Noumenon."

Thus, apparently, Berkeley's idealism is not only a common-sense philosophy, but eminently realistic. But there still remains the question about the source of perception. What causes it? His answer, though very dogmatic, is not convincing. He maintains that "our ideas are produced in us conformably with the laws of nature. These laws have been ordained by God. To suppose that matter is the mere occasional cause—the vehicle through which the laws of nature operate—is gratuitous. The existence of matter cannot be established either by intuition or by inference; the notion is full of contradictions. Whereas the existence of spirit is known directly; and spirit is God. The agency of the Creator is therefore more simple and direct. He had no need of creating first laws, and afterwards matter, through which these laws should come into effect. He thought, and his thought reflected itself in us directly without the superfluous aid of matter as a mere go-between."*

Berkeley thus liquidated philosophy in order to combat materialism. His idealism is no philosophy; it is a mere reassertion of theology. Having arbitrarily denied the objective existence of matter, he goes on to disprove the objective existence of "things directly perceived". "What are the objects but the things which we perceive by sense?" This is a very plausible attitude. But the next question is a dogmatic assertion. "And what do we perceive besides our ideas or sensations?" In the absence of scientific psychology, the answer to this question would be necessarily ambiguous. That ambiguity was seized upon by idealism, and Berkeley triumphantly challenged: "Is it not plainly repugnant that anyone of these ideas should exist unperceived?" It is evident how he confuses ideas with things. Materialism does not maintain that ideas exist objectively outside of our mind. That is a contention of the oldest form of idealism—Platonism.

The critical aspect of Berkeley's doctrine, however, is very cogent, thanks to the half-heartedness of the Sensationalist materialism. He argued: "The substratum, confessedly unknown, is a mere abstraction. If it is unknown and unknowable, it is a figment. It is a figment worse than useless. It is pernicious, as the basis of all atheism. If by matter

* "Treatise Concerning the Principles of Human Knowledge"

you understand that which is seen, felt, tasted and touched, then, I say matter exists. If, on the contrary, you understand by matter that occult substance which is not seen, not felt, not tasted and not touched, that of which the senses do not, cannot, inform you—then, I say I don't believe in matter."

The militant Bishop took advantage of the timidity of his opponents and turned the tables against them. But to-day, his arguments have no force. To-day, the existence of matter is no longer relegated to the region of the occult; it is a perfectly known and knowable substance. The reflection could be considered as the only reality, so long as the things reflected were declared to be unknown, and even unknowable. In that backward state of the theory of cognition, it was not possible to assert that the sense-perceptions were true reflections of outside objects. By removing all possible doubt regarding the objective reality of the outside world, experimental science has knocked the ground under the feet of idealism.

Berkeley was eminently practical. He did not deny the existence of things which are immediately perceived. He waged war against the Cartesian and Spinozist conception of substance which lends itself to the theory of a material substratum as the origin of everything. That basis of materialist philosophy Berkeley desired to destroy, and replace it by a Divine Will as the cause of everything. But once the existence of immediately perceptible things is admitted, a common source of their origin is a logical conclusion. Therefore, he argued: "I do not argue against the existence of any one thing that we can apprehend either by sensation or reflection. That the things I see with my eyes and touch with my hands do exist, really exist, I make not the least question. The only thing whose existence I deny, is that which philosophers call matter or corporeal substance." The fallacy of the argument is obvious. The things exist, but not the substance out of which they are made. The things are there, simply because God has caused them to be there. That is no philosophy.

Berkeley was correct to hold that, in the absence of mind, no perception is possible; that is to say, in that case, outside objects are practically non-existent. A stone has no perception of a tree. Therefore, the one cannot be conscious of the other. All this is very simple. But the counter-part of this correct and simple view is altogether false. The inability of the stone to perceive the existence of the tree does not sweep the latter out of the world of objective being. Perceptions are dependent upon our senses; ideation is a property of the brain; but it does not follow therefrom that perceptions and ideas are purely mental phenomena, independent of things objectively existing outside. Still, this is what Berkeley maintained.

If you admit that the table, stone, tree, etc., really exist, you cannot avoid the logical necessity of reducing them all to a common source of origin, unless you are prepared to abandon all claim to scientific thought. Berkeley could not be expected to do so, and still pretend to be a philosopher. He did reduce the complex to a simple, the particular to a general, the many to one, the diversity to unity;

only he traced the origin of material things—table, stone, tree etc.—to a "spiritual substance". So, his whole philosophy is based upon the prejudice of creation out of nothing. Material things are made out of spirit—conjured out of nothing. Full-fledged idealism, which does not bother to be practical or be guided by common-sense, is more logical, more scientific than this crude magic. It boldly denies that anything exists but absolute idea, and declares the phenomenal world as illusion, hallucination or at best "expression of the idea" (Hegel). But, first to admit the material existence of particular things, and then deny a material substratum of them all, is a stupendous absurdity. The trick by which Berkeley seeks to make this absurdity appear plausible, does not convince anyone except those who believe in a permanent miracle.

My knowledge of the table is conditional upon its sensible qualities; my idea of it is formed out of the image it throws on the retina of my eyes; so, I must be satisfied with the image, call it the real thing, and let the table itself get dissolved into its "spiritual substratum"! That is the substance of Berkeley's philosophy. And all the diverse schools of modern scientific idealism still stick to that position in one way or other.

In his zeal to endow faith with a deceptive shine of philosophy and reason, Berkeley went a bit too far and ruined his whole system. He argued: "The *esse* (being) of every idea is perception; it is not possible to separate, even in thought, any of our ideas from perception; their being consists in being perceived."

Now, perception, which is the essence of ideas, implies the existence of a thing perceived. Granting that our ideas are not exact representations or images of the things, the objective existence of the latter is by no means disproved. It is simply silly to endow the shadow with reality on the plea that we do not know the substance fully well. Philosophy should rather set about the task of finding the ways and means of knowing the substance, and test the veracity of the shadow by the standard of the knowledge of the substance. That is, philosophy should reject speculation as an inadequate means of acquiring knowledge, and strengthen itself with the help of experimental science.

The basic contradiction of Berkeley's philosophy is that it reinforces the doctrine of the identity of thought and being, a doctrine which destroys idealism. This basic contradiction of the system is overcome by reconciling the reality of the existence of immediately perceptible things with the doctrine of a spiritual substance as their common substratum. Things do not exist except in, perception. This doctrine would lead to such absurdity as to maintain that the New World did not exist before Columbus discovered it. Berkeley avoids such an absurd consequence by an equally absurd expedience.—the eternal perception by the eternal spirit. So, things, after all, do not exist actually, except as bubbles in the ocean of the eternal spirit. This, therefore, is the real being, and the rest is fleeting phenomena.

Liberated from the assumption of the "eternal spirit", these arguments of Berkeley lead to atheism against which he was waging the war. "All our knowledge of objects is a knowledge of ideas; objects and ideas are the same; therefore, nothing exists but what is perceived."

Materialism fully agrees with this conclusion, but turns it as a deadly weapon against Berkeley's idealism. Neither God nor eternal spirit exists, because it cannot be perceived by man. Since the whole system of Berkeley rested precariously on the belief in the existence of God and the eternal spirit, by disproving their existence, it destroys itself.

Berkeley's system, as all non-materialist philosophy, stands or falls with the conception of consciousness. It has a logical appearance as long as consciousness is admitted to be an independent entity or function or property, antecedent to perception, the latter affecting it immediately. But deny such an *a priori* consciousness, as the knowledge of modern physiology forces you to do, and idealism becomes an absurdity. Because, consciousness is nothing but the sum total of sense-perceptions; it is the immediate result of external influences upon an organism. Mind is not an independent entity. It is simply a property of organic matter.

The credit of having freed philosophy from the unhealthy atmosphere of dualism, belongs to Berkeley. All the modern philosophers before him were tied to scholasticism by the bond of dualism. By replacing the material substratum of the world with the "spiritual substance", and identifying it with God, Berkeley discarded dualism. In consequence, the issue between idealism and materialism became sharper than ever. Idealism, as a monist philosophy, developed magnificently and tried to overcome its antagonist; but freed from dualism, it had no basis. The only serious opposition to materialism is the doctrine of creation. Idealism cannot subscribe to the doctrine of something coming out of nothing without giving up the claim to be philosophy. By developing the monist conception of the world to the extreme of pantheism, it merges itself into materialism. That was done later by Spinoza.

The other great exponent of a modern school of metaphysics is Kant. But he decidedly disagreed with the view that the phenomenal world is the product of our ideas. Very significantly, he characterises Berkeley as looking for a new prop for his distressed faith. Though known as the founder of the school of "Transcendental Idealism", Kant, in reality, made great contributions to the development of materialism. The very foundation of his philosophy was materialistic. Primarily a mathematician, he was profoundly influenced by Newton, whose mechanistic view of the Universe culminated in the Nebular Theory associated with the name of Kant and the French mathematician Laplace. About Kant's great achievement in this respect, the famous German astronomer Hemlholtz wrote: "It was Kant who, feeling great interest in the physical description of the earth, and the planetary system, had undertaken the laborious study of the works of Newton; and as an evidence of the depth to which he had penetrated into the fundamental ideas of Newton, seized the masterly idea that the same attractive force of all ponderable matter, which now supports the motion of the planets, must also aforetime have been able to form the planetary system from matters loosely scattered in space."

In his most important work, "General History of Nature and Theory of the Heavens", Kant proposed "to discuss the constitution and the mechanical origin of the whole Universe, according to Newton's principles, and to explain them mechanically by the natural course of development, to the exclusion of all miracles."

With such a view of the origin of the Universe, one could not possibly tolerate religious prejudices and dogmas on the basic question regarding the relation between man and nature. The Nebular Theory of Kant definitely disposed of the Creator. When Kant set out to reform philosophy by combating metaphysics, he undertook, objectively and historically, no other task than to drive religious faiths out of their "scientific and philosophical" entrenchments. The "Critique of Pure Reason" was an attack upon the lingering faith in a super-natural, super-sensual force.

The cardinal principle of Kant's philosophy is that all knowledge is necessarily based upon experience; there is no eternal truth, no absolute idea. There is very little difference with materialism. Kant himself emphasises the materialist point of departure of his philosophy. "The proposition of all genuine idealists, from the Eleatic school to Bishop Berkeley, is stated in the formula that all cognition through sense and experience is mere appearance; the truth can be reached only through pure understanding and Pure Reason. The principle governing my idealism is: all cognition through pure understanding and Pure Reason is nothing but appearance, and truth is in experience only."* Kant characterises the so-called cognition through Pure Reason as "the dangerous province of creation out of nothing—wide and stormy ocean, the true home of mirage." He further maintains that "all ideas that seek to penetrate the sphere beyond our experience are mere delusions."

Having subjected the Pure Reason of metaphysics to his "all-shattering criticism", Kant proceeds to build up not only a new system of metaphysics, but actually lays the foundation of a new religion. The postulate of the "thing-in-itself", and the "categorical imperatives" are arbitrarily built super-structures which cannot be reconciled with the clearly materialistic foundation of Kant's philosophy. As a philosopher, he was a materialist; but as the prophet of a new religion, he had to fall back upon illusions and fantasies which he himself had combated as a philosopher. So very contradictory are the two parts of Kant's philosophy, that a learned Kantian is constrained to write:

"That there exist things in themselves, which have a spaceless and timeless existence, Kant could never prove to us out of his principles, for that would be transcendental, even though negative knowledge of the properties of the things in themselves, and such a knowledge, on Kant's own theory, is entirely impossible."

In order to avoid carrying his critical thought to its logical consequences, Kant took refuge in scep-

* "Prologomena".
‡ Lange, "History of Materialism".

ticism—the convenient harbour for all shame-faced materialists. Through his lapse into scepticism, which so flagrantly ill-fits the critical mind of the "reformer of philosophy", Kant changes the whole nature of his system. It is his *salto mortale.* He accomplishes the task of freeing philosophy from the domination of theology; but on the other hand, brings the Supreme Being out of the museum of history and places it beyond the pretensions of experimental reason to which he grants supremacy in the phenomenal world.

The repudiation of the super-natural in human knowledge was the point of departure of Kant's philosophy. It necessarily led up to the alternatives of scepticism and materialism. Scepticism is a negative point of view; no philosophical system can be built upon a negative principle. If one cannot decidedly discard faith, he is sure to relapse into it sooner or later. Then, faith is transformed into something "positive", in the shape of "mystical morality" or pantheism. Both these grew out of Kant's philosophy. He himself founded a new system of mystical morality with transcendental sanctions. The latter course was followed by his disciple Schopenhauer.

The negative outcome of Kant's philosophy was determined by the conditions of his time. Socially, Germany was more backward than England and France, where materialism made tremendous headway in the seventeenth and eighteenth century. In the latter two countries, the bourgeoisie were ready to undertake the building of a new social order. In Germany, they were not yet ready for the task. Since the stormy days of the Reformation, the country laid exhausted. Economic life was practically stagnant. The positive outcome of the great Peasant War had been the strengthening of the petty princes who exercised their feudal power and privileges, ruining the country economically as well as politically. There was no striving for a National State in antagonism to the Universal Power of the Church and its secular arm, the Holy Roman Empire. Nevertheless, the shock of the Great French Revolution was felt also in Germany. The enlightenment radiated from France and penetrated the sluggish darkness of Central Europe. Kant was a result thereof. But he could not rise above the conditions in which he lived. His thoughts were determined by them. From the very beginning, Kant fought on two fronts,—against scholastic metaphysics, which obstructed social progress, and, on the other hand, against materialism which would eventually create a revolutionary ferment among the people. In the preface to the second edition of the "Critique of Pure Reason", he had written: "I cannot recognise God, freedom and immortality as necessary for any practical use for my reason." Yet, towards the end of his life, he declared: "I must curb knowledge in order to find room for faith."

He further wrote: "The mortal life must always be brightened by the hope of a future existence. Only this way it will be possible to root out materialism, fatalism, atheism, free-thinking, disbelief, dreams and superstitions, which are likely to be generally harmful." That may be taken as a declaration of faith; but this confusion of everything also indicates a deplorable mental degeneration on the part of the "all-shattering" critic.

The historical necessity of materialism, however, was proved by Kant himself, who, in order to fight the potential enemy, had to build up a philosophical system clearly on a materialistic foundation. When it becomes necessary to use materialism for fighting materialism, only the imperiousness of materialism is established. The sophistic super-structure of Kant's philosophy has been relegated to the dusty shelf of the Classics. But its materialist foundation stands firm as a mile-stone of the intellectual progress of modern times. Every great thinker, who contributed anything permanent to human progress, advanced the cause of materialism, even if he were an avowed enemy of materialism. This proves that materialism is the driving force of all human progress.

The greatest of modern idealist philosophers, Hegel, liquidated idealism by developing it to its logical conclusion. His Absolute Idealism freed philosophy from the fallacy of dualism, and established a monism which was either pantheism or materialism. Hegel rejected the Kantian doctrine of the thing-in-itself. "The thing in itself is the empty abstraction from all conditions, and just because it is thus removed from all conditions, it is removed from all knowledge." He maintains that "the phenomenon is not the unsubstantial phantom of an unknowable, but its actual manifestation—the reality of the essence."

Idealist philosophy previously (Leibniz, Berkeley, Fichte and Schelling) traced the root of idea to something external,—"pre-established harmony", "action of deity", "impulse" or "intellectual intuition". Hegel shattered the dualism which had thus vitiated idealism, by making his "notion" the self-existing primary element. It is something like Spinoza's substance. So, God or a super-natural source of the Universe was eliminated; metaphysical speculation committed suicide. Nevertheless, Hegel was not free from the prejudice of God; but he placed that unnecessary adjunct at the tail-end of things. The Universe is not the product of God. God comes into being only when the Absolute Idea has finished its process of self-development. God comes into existence when "notion" develops itself into self-consciousness. So, the God is a creation of Hegel. There could be no more conclusive proof of the old dictum that man makes God after his own image. The implication of the Hegelian conception of God is very far-reaching. Firstly, God does not exist objectively. The conception is a result of the evolution of thought. Secondly, "notion" realises into self-consciousness in every individual. The man becomes God, no longer bound by the process of nature. Nature is there for him no longer to wonder at and speculate about, but to conquer. The magnificent suicide of classical idealistic philosophy celebrates the final triumph of materialism.

Hegel rejects the vulgar theological notion that God created the world. He holds that the creation is not an act, but an eternal movement,—not a thing done, but a perpetual process of becoming. This is not creation out of nothing. It is as if nothing becoming something. And this apparent paradox is possible because nothing and something (in the state of unconditionedness) are identical. In plain scientific language, Hegel's doctrine means, if it means anything, that creation is simply an eternal process of evolution out of a primal existence which contains the germs of everything.

While liquidating the idealist philosophy, Hegel also laid down certain tremendously revolutionary principles of a new philosophy. He declared: "Everything real is rational; and everything rational is real." But Hegel does not consider everything in existence to be real, unconditionally. According to him, reality is an attribute only of what is necessary at the same time. "Reality of a thing is demonstrated by its being necessary." What is necessary is, in the last analysis, always found to be rational. So, necessity is the ultimate standard. As long as a thing is necessary, it is rational; and so long as it is rational, it is a reality. The corollary to this is: As soon as a thing ceases to be necessary, it is no longer rational, and therefore forfeits the right to exist. Moreover, the character of reality does not belong to any social or political order under all conditions and in all times. That is to say, something real to-day becomes unreal in course of time, under altered circumstances. In their respective times, and the given conditions, both things are equally real, and rational in so far as they are necessary. But judged by the constantly changing standard of necessity, the old reality ceases to be rational and thus becomes unreal, to be replaced by the new reality which is rational because of its being necessary. The Roman Republic, for example, was real; so also was the Roman Empire which replaced it. In course of evolution, a real thing loses its reality, because it ceases to be necessary. It becomes irrational, and must be replaced by a new thing which is rational and real, because it has become necessary. So continues the process *ad infinitum*. This is the Hegelian dialectic law of history.

It was for Marx and Engels to appreciate this positive outcome of Hegel's philosophy as the "algebra of revolution". Science provided the materialist philosophy with a solid foundation of the knowledge of nature. The evolution of pure thought, on the other hand, culminated in the formulation of a new method of reasoning—the dialectic logic, which reinforced materialism logically. Modern materialism thus triumphed as the inevitable outcome of the entire process of intellectual development ever since the dawn of history. It is the greatest human heritage.

# CHAPTER V

## MODERN MATERIALISM

IT must be clear from the foregoing chapters that materialism is not what it is vulgarly called, namely, the cult of "eat, drink and be merry". It is the explanation of the world without the assumption of anything super-natural. The efforts made throughout the ages for such an explanation have established a monistic view of the Universe, and revealed the substratum of everything—body, mind, soul—as a material substance, a physical entity, largely known and progressively knowable: Existence precedes thought; things ideas; matter spirit.

Idealistic philosophy reverses the relation. But the antithesis of philosophical materialism can no longer be stated in religious terms. That would be too absurd, in the age of scientific knowledge and rationalist mode of thought. A philosophical controversy must be conducted on a philosophical plane—with a philosophical terminology. Therefore, in modern times, spiritualism takes the arena against materialism in the deceptive garb of the idealist philosophy, which has been aptly characterised by Feuerbach as "philosophical spiritualism". The issue of the controversy has been reduced to epistemology: Reality or unreality of the material world, and the possibility of human mind to know it.

The materialist point of view that the world exists objectively, by itself, independent and irrespective of its being perceived by human consciousness, dislodges this latter from the place of primacy. This basic principle of Materialism could not be conclusively established except upon the firm foundation of the discoveries of modern science in the eighteenth and nineteenth centuries. On the other hand, the bold speculations and ingenious hypotheses of the rationalist and materialist thinkers ever since the Renaissance encouraged scientific enquiry. The cooperation of materialist thought and experimental science bore magnificent fruits in the eighteenth century.

The great materialist thinkers of the seventeenth century held that our ideas were but abstractions of the images of external objects, received by the senses, and that the external objects were thus unconditionally knowable. The French Encyclopedists, in the following century, called "those, who, conscious only of their own existence and of a succession of external sensations, do not admit anything else, protagonists of an extravagant system—the off-spring of blindness itself." (Diderot). The Encyclopedists definitely held the view that our senses gave us true representations of outside objects, and sense-perceptions were the only source of ideas. According to them, sensation is a property of organic matter.* That view, yet only a conjecture at that time, was later on corroborated by the empirical investigations of the great Naturalists of the nineteenth century.

In 1758 appeared the great work of Helvetius, "The Mind". It was the greatest treatise on ethics

* Dialogue of D'Alembert and Diderot.

produced in the eighteenth century, and France led the thought of Europe in that period. The basic principles enunciated therein were the following. It is an incontestable fact that the difference between man and other animals is the result of a difference in their external form; that the structure of our body is the sole cause of our boasted superiority. This becomes evident when it is considered that thought is the product of two faculties common to man and other animals, namely, the faculty of receiving impressions from external objects, and the faculty of remembering those impressions. All essential principles of our moral actions are deduced from this position; all notions of duty and virtue must be tested by their relation to senses; in other words, by the gross amount of physical enjoyment to which they give rise. This is the true basis of moral philosophy. The alternative view of moral, to be deceived by conventional expressions, has no other foundation except prejudice, born of ignorance.

Condillac was the greatest metaphysician of the century. He was a materialist. "He found it utterly impossible to escape from those (materialist) tendencies towards the external world that governed his age."* In his famous "Treatise on Sensations", he asserts that everything we know is the result of sensations, by which he means the effect produced on us by the action of the external world. With some looseness of expression, and perhaps some looseness of thought, Locke had assumed the separate existence of a power of reflection, and believed that, by means of

* Buckle, "History of Civilisation'.

that mysterious power, the product of sensations became available. He used the term 'reflection' so vaguely as to "allow his disciples to make of his doctrine what they pleased."* Moved by the prevailing temper of his time, Condillac would not admit any such distinction between sensation and reflection. He rejected the faculty of reflection as a source of ideas. He held that reflection partly is the channel, through which ideas run from the senses, and that partly, in its origin, it is itself a sensation. He was definitely of the opinion that the faculties of man were solely caused by the operation of his senses. He argues that the judgments we form are ascribed to a divine influence, because it is a convenient mode of reasoning which has arisen from the difficulty of analysing them. By considering how our judgments actually arise we can remove those obscurities. "In man, nature is the beginning of all, to nature we owe the whole of our knowledge. We instruct ourselves according to her lessons. The entire act of reasoning consists in continuing the work which she has appointed us to perform."

The philosophical revolution, brought about by the bold materialistic doctrines of the French Encyclopedists, directly led to a tremendous advance of positive knowledge. The consequence of the growth of materialist thought has been described as follows:

"It was this dangerous, but plausible, principle which drew the attention of men from the Church to the State; which was seen in Helvetius, the most celebrated of the French moralists, and in Condillac, the most celebrated of the French metaphysicians.

* Whewell, 'History of Moral Philosophy".

It was this same principle which, by increasing the reputation of Nature, induced the ablest thinkers to devote themselves to a study of her laws, and to abandon those other pursuits which had been popular in the preceding age. In consequence of this movement, such wonderful additions were made to every branch of physical science that more new truths concerning the external world were discovered in France during the latter half of the eighteenth century than during all the previous periods together."*

Epoch-making discoveries regarding the nature of heat, light, electricity and magnetism were made by Provost, Dulong, Fourier, D'Alibard, Coulomb, Frensel and a whole host of other lesser lights—all in the latter part of the eighteenth century. Modern chemistry was also created by French materialism in that period of great intellectual outburst. The father of this science, Lavoisier, lived in that period, together with other famous chemists like Fourcroy, de Morveau, Verdeil, etc. That was the age of great Buffon and Cuvier—founders of geology, zoology, anatomy, physiology and botany also received great impetus. Cuvier and Bichat are the fathers of biology. Cabanis founded modern physiology and psychology. Appreciating the achievements of those great scientists, all inspired by materialist thought, Buckle writes:

"By this union of geology and anatomy, there was first introduced into the study of nature a clear conception of the magnificent doctrine of universal change; while at the same time, there grew up by its

* Buckle, "History of Civilisation".

side a conception equally steady of the regularity with which the changes are accomplished, and of the undeviating laws by which they are governed. Similar ideas have no doubt been held in preceding ages; but the great Frenchmen of the eighteenth century were the first to apply them to the entire structure of the globe, and who thus prepared the way for that still higher view to which in our time the most advanced thinkers are rapidly rising. For it is now beginning to be understood that, since every addition to knowledge, affords fresh proof of the regularity with which all the changes of nature are conducted, we are bound to believe that the same regularity existed long before our little planet assumed its present form, and long before man trod the surface of the earth."*

In the nineteenth century, science, with its all-conquering methods, steadily advanced farther, drawing more and more subjects under its rule, yielding answers to more and more problems, while theology and metaphysics remained impotent to furnish convincing answers and were found constantly to be in flagrant contradiction with the certainties of experience. Of the three modes of explaining phenomena—theological, metaphysical and scientific—the latter gained strength daily. Previously, all men had accepted the theological explanation of the world and society. But in proportion as knowledge advanced, that explanation was discovered to be incessantly in contradiction with experience. As knowledge advanced, men withdrew more and more phenomena from the protection of supernatural agen-

* Buckle, "History of Civilisation."

cies, and placed them under the jurisdiction of the mechanistic laws of nature; gods and supernatural entities were deposed for good.

In 1809, Lorenz Oken wrote his "Manual of the Philosophy of Nature", in which he advanced the theory that the phenomenon of life in all organisms originates in a common chemical substance. The theory of evolution by biological use and disuse had been suggested by Lamarck even before that. In 1815 was published Lamarck's "Natural History" which first introduced the term 'biology'. Lamarck wrote: "Life is purely a physical phenomenon. All the phenomena of life depend on mechanical, physical and chemical causes which are inherent in the nature of matter itself. The simplest animal and the simplest plants, which stand at the lowest point in the scale of organisation, have originated and still originate by spontaneous generation. All animate natural bodies or organisms are subject to the same laws as inanimate natural bodies. The ideas and actions of the understanding are motional phenomena of the central nervous system. The will is never free."

The investigation initiated by the bold hypotheses of Lamarck and Oken led to positively revolutionary discoveries. Darwin immensely improved the Lamarckian theory of descent with the doctrine of natural selection. The clear and unavoidable implications of Darwinism left absolutely no room for a Creator, and consequently for the traditional religious prejudices, nor for the speculation about a spiritual essence of the Universe. Darwinism was the object of a bitter attack by the Church, theologists, pious philosophers and even by many scientists of the time. Darwin was damned as the "greatest atheist". He himself was staggered by the revolutionary implications of his great scientific discoveries. But once ideas are created, they move with their own momentum. In spite of Darwin's ambiguous attitude regarding the philosophical implications of his scientific discoveries they asserted themselves through the work of his disciples. Haeckel, for example found sufficient ground for the assumption that there is "in the foundation-stones of the structure of matter itself a property similar to sensation." Other eminent biologists, pursuing their own line of research, arrived at similar conclusions, in the light of which the principles of materialist epistemology came out of the domains of hypothetical conjecture, to be established as empirically verified philosophical concepts.

Scientific knowledge about the history of the Universe shows that organic beings did not exist on this earth from eternity. They could not, owing to the uninhabitable state of this planet as well as the other members of the solar system. Only at a certain stage of the physical growth of the earth, organisms came into being. The theories of descent and natural selection can be traced back to that remote point in the history of our globe. Then arises the question: How did the first organism grow? The German scientist Haeckel was the first to raise the question boldly, and answer it with the hypothesis of spontaneous generation. "This is the point at which most naturalists, even at the present day, are inclined to give up the attempt at natural explanation, and take refuge in the miracle of an inconceivable creation. In doing so, they quit the domain of scientific knowledge, and renounce all further insight into the eternal laws which have determined nature's history. But before despondingly taking such a step, and before we despair of the possibility of any knowledge of this important process, we may at least make an attempt to understand it."*

Haeckel himself held the key to the problem which he so modestly approached. It was in his discovery of the very simplest form of organism which he described as "organisms without organs". He discovered them floating on the sea-water. "They are very small living corpuscles which strictly speaking do not deserve the name of organism, not compound of any organs at all, but consist entirely of shapeless, simple, homogeneous matter. The body of one of these is nothing more than a shapeless, mobile, little lump of mucus or slime, consisting of an albuminous combination of carbon. Simpler or more imperfect organisms we cannot possibly conceive."†

The English scientist Thomas Huxley also discovered a similar form of lowest organism in the depths of the ocean. His hypothesis having thus been verified by independent discovery, Haeckel wrote: "On account of the perfect homogeneity of the albuminous substance of their bodies, on account of their utter want of heterogeneous particles, these are more closely connected with anorgana than with organism, and evidently form the transition between

* Ernst Haeckel, "The History of Creation."
† Ernst Haeckel, "General Morphology."

the inorganic and the organic worlds of bodies, as is necessitated by the hypothesis of spontaneous generation."

The discovery of these simplest and lowest organisms threw light upon the secrets of life. No room was left for the persistent tradition or superstition about the miraculous origin of life. The hypothesis of spontaneous generation was verified. In the time of Lamarck and later on, the probability of the hypothesis was doubted, because the lowest known forms of organism were of relatively composite nature. But the primitive forms discovered by Haeckel and Huxley were not composite organisms, not aggregates of several organs; they "consist solely of a single chemical combination, and yet grow, nourish and propagate themselves." (Haeckel). So, a simple compound of carbon was found to be the seed of original life,—the totality of the molecular motion of matter, which, in higher forms of organisms, is endowed with the dignity of the mysterious super-natural "vital force" (soul). Since then, organic chemistry discovered that the most elementary substratum, which brings into evidence the play of the mysterious vital force, was a combination of carbon with oxygen, hydrogen and nitrogen. This "material" play-ground of the super-natural vital force is an albuminous substance. Originally, all organisms are simple lumps of such albuminous formations, called protoplasm.

There is no difference between the organic and inorganic matter. All living bodies are formed out of such chemical elements as carbon, oxygen, hydrogen, nitrogen, sulphur, potassium, sodium etc. No such elements have been found in vegetable and animal bodies as are absent in the inorganic substances. When a certain combination of a number of chemical elements produces the phenomenon of life, it enters into the organic domain. The primary manifestation of this phenomenon is the process of nutrition and multiplication.

By boldly establishing the Lamarckian hypothesis of spontaneous generation, Haeckel completed Darwinism as a pillar of the modern materialist philosophy. He wrote: "A conception of an immaterial force, which at first creates matter, is an article of faith which has nothing whatsoever to do with human science. Where faith commences, science ends. These two arts of human mind must strictly be kept apart from each other. Faith has its origin in the poetic imagination; knowledge, on the other hand, originates in the reason and intelligence of man. Science has to pluck the blessed fruits from the tree of knowledge, unconcerned whether these conquests trench upon the poetical imaginings of faith or not." Darwinism, elaborated by Haeckel and subsequently by a number of other scientists, provided an unshakable foundation of knowledge to materialist philosophy.

Yet, whenever and wherever science failed to give fully satisfactory explanations of all the phenomena, man continued to place reliance upon supernatural and spiritual agencies, supposing them to be beyond the reach of science, and maintaining in consequence that even the defective and imperfect scientific knowledge, which can never attain the absolute truth, was possible only owing to the "divine spark" in man. The inscrutable will and invisible hand of the All-Mighty were triumphantly detected wherever the mechanistic laws of nature were not yet discovered, or the operation of them appeared to be suspended by the intervention of unforeseen factors. Ignorance became the shrine of God, the decisive argument in favour of religion. Hence, we come across minds completely dominated by the scientific outlook in astronomical, physical and chemical questions, nevertheless stubbornly refusing to apply the same mechanistic principles to the investigation of the organic world, particularly to man. Biology and psychology still remain confused by theological and metaphysical prejudices, although the nineteenth century is crowded with positively revolutionary discoveries of natural science in the organic as well as in the inorganic world. Particularly, to history, politics, law, economics and ethics, was the application of mechanistic laws and the inductive method of investigation deprecated even by "scientific men", as dogmatic, perverse, disruptive, reprehensible and unscientific.

It is, however, no paradox that so many scientifically minded men, even scientists, should linger under the waning influence of the religious and metaphysical view of life. The cause of the apparent paradox is to be found in the specialisation of scientific study. It was necessary for particular groups of men to devote themselves wholely to particular branches of science—to small, limited fields of investigation which were but minute fractions of the vast domain of nature. The result was that the sole occupation with particular groups of phenomena made the average man of science lose sight of the comprehensive nature of science as a whole. They failed to see the forest for the trees, as it were. The very creditable and profusely productive zeal of practice in detail eclipsed the broad vision of theory. In short, specialised men of science were not able to draw broad philosophical conclusions from their own discoveries and knowledge. The co-ordination of the vast knowledge acquired by the diverse branches of science was to be done by a new philosophy—materialism.

Bishop Berkeley began his crusade against materialism with the following declaration: "The doctrine of matter or corporeal substance is the main pillar and support of Scepticism, upon the same foundation have been raised all the impious schemes of atheism and irreligion. How great a friend 'material substance' has been to the atheists in all ages, is needless to relate. Matter being once expelled out of nature, drags with it so many sceptical and impious notions, such as incredible amount and number of disputes and puzzling questions, which have been thorns in the side of divines as well as philosophers." The indignant divine concludes his passionate denunciation of materialism with the pious conviction that "all friends of knowledge, peace and religion would surely wish that my arguments have completely demolished the enemy."

But that was not to be. Religion was defeated by knowledge. Even in the plausible form of "scientific" idealism, it could not hold its own against the quintessence of human knowledge—philosophical materialism. The discoveries in the field of geology, palaeontology, astronomy, chemistry, physics, biology, since the days of Berkeley, made it a matter of common knowledge that the physical existence of the Universe preceded the appearance of man by ages of incalculable duration. The Universe is composed of a countless multitude of stars, of which the sun is one, and the earth is only a satellite of the sun. A little contemplation of these facts makes it evident how insignificant a factor human consciousness is.

The comparative insignificance of human consciousness, however, is only quantitative. Qualitatively, its importance is immense. That is demonstrated by the very ability to acquire the knowledge which lays bare its quantitative insignificance in comparison with the vast background of the physical being. Having grown out of matter, the spirit dominates matter. The epic of the struggle for this domination is the history of man. The consciousness of the comparative, qualitative, insignificance of the spirit—the recognition of the fact of its subordination to matter—generally does not, in the least, underestimate its unlimited potentiality, cannot belittle the glory of its achievements in the realm of positive knowledge. On the contrary, this recognition sets human spirit really free by liberating it from the fetters of teleology. For the first time, human spirit (call it soul, if you please) stands on its own legs, shines not as the reflection of an unseen light, but in the native effulgence of its own being. When man feels the endless potentialities of his own mind, the genesis of which is no metaphysical mystery, it is no longer necessary for him to believe in any supernatural force governing his destiny or guiding his footsteps.

The knowledge that life occupies such an insignificant place in the physical vastness of the Universe, reveals the absurdity of the teleological conception of religion, that everything happens according to a divine purpose. Whatever religious view you may take, be it the mosaic doctrine of creation, or the pantheistic idea of emanation (Vedanta), the man occupies the centre of the stage. Either God created the world for the benefit of the man, or the purpose of the whole scheme of the Universe is to provide a stage-setting for the whimsical peregrinations of the soul. Both these doctrines, together with the numerous variations of each, are shattered by the discovery that life, in any form, occupies an infinitesimal small place in the order of the physical Universe, and is scarcely a minute old compared to the incalculable age of its material background.

God does not appear to be the omnipotent and omniscient master-builder as believed by religious men. If, in order to create the tiny speck of dirt inhabited by crawling bits of carbo-hydrates, he had to waste the immeasurable mass of matter constituting the Universe, and spend the incalculable trillions of years in that superb feat of wastefulness, he has certainly not as much ability or power or intelligence as any mortal architect or structural engineer. No intelligent man can accept such a God as the arbitrary mentor of his destiny. It is simply absurd. Had the Universe been created by an omnipotent and omniscient God for the benefit of man, the latter would have been given a higher place in

16

it. As regards the pantheistic religious view (Vedantism), it is equally absurd. How could the Universe be the play-ground of the soul, since it existed through countless ages without any trace of life? In the absence of life, in any form, there can be no consciousness which is detected in organic matter only in a comparatively high level of evolution. In the absence of consciousness, there cannot be any question of an intelligent purpose. The physical Universe is, indeed, governed by definite laws, but, being in an entirely lifeless state, cannot be the vehicle of an intelligent purpose. Its laws are purely mechanistic, being but variations of motion inseparable from the existence of matter. The natural history of the earth again proves conclusively that intelligence is a comparatively new phenomenon of living matter, which is nothing more mysterious than inanimate matter subjected to certain physico-chemical processes. Throughout the entire scheme of the Universe, there is to be found neither the hand of the all-mighty God nor any intelligent purpose.

Thus, Berkeley was perfectly correct in attacking materialist epistemology as the repugnant source of atheism and irreligion. The recogintion of the objective reality of things, reduceable to a common material denominator, sounds the death-knell of religion, faith, metaphysics and mysticism. If the world of individual perception is independent of, and prior to, the individual ego (soul), then, the conclusion is irresistible that the world of universal perception is equally independent of, and prior to, the imaginary Universal Ego (God). Soul and God are inseparable twins. They must stand or fall together. This materialistic deduction of pure thought has now been empirically corroborated. Materialism has become more than a plausible hypothesis; it is a verified scientific theory.

A pupil of Hegel, Feuerbach came to the conclusion that the Absolute Idealism of his teacher was the highest culmination of classical philosophy, and held that, for the future, philosophy must strike out a new path. He stated the cardinal principles of the "New Philosophy" in the following memorable words: "Thought is conditioned by existence, not existence by thought. Being is self-determined, has its foundation in itself." The traditionally believed relation between soul and body, mind and matter, is here reversed. Religious and metaphysical categories, such as God, Soul, First Principle, Final Cause, did not create man, but they are the creations of man. This thesis was brilliantly elaborated in Feuerbach's great work, "The Essence of Christianity". It is a master-piece of religious criticism, applicable theoretically to all religions.

The following is the summary of Feuerbach's New Philosophy: "The material world is accessible to our senses. The world to which we belong is the only real world; our consciousness and our thought are engendered by material organ (brain)—a part of the body. Matter is not created by spirit; spirit itself is but the highest product of matter." Feuerbach made full use of the Hegelian criticism of the cult of the "thing-in-itself"—the last refuge of metaphysics and therefore of religion. Hegel said: "If you know all the qualities of a thing, you know the thing in itself; nothing remains but the fact that the said thing exists outside us; and when your senses have taught you that fact, you have grasped the last remnant of the thing in itself." These words of the greatest and most consistent modern idealist philosopher forecast many discoveries of the natural sciences and were pregnant with the germs of the materialist epistemology which were to fructify so magnificently under the care of his great pupils—Feuerbach, Marx and Engels.

In the place of the time-honoured religious theological and metaphysical dogmas, Feuerbach placed the man—of flesh and blood—in the centre of things, and proceeded to interpret everything, including those dogmas, by that standard. That was an all-shattering method. Everything appeared in a new light. The clay-feet of old gods were exposed. The human essence of divine conceptions was laid bare. Theological mysteries were revealed as the result of anthropomorphical preoccupations. The carnal core of religion was discovered. Faith was found to be the expression of egoism. In short, Feuerbach's materialist criticism pulled down the religio-theo-metaphysical super-structure of civilisation, not only Western, but as a whole. His criticism was not historical, but theoretical, equally applicable to any particular subject. But Feuerbach's philosophy was not without a flaw. It was in its point of departure, in his failure to see things in a process. The being of man determines his consciousness, and being is governed by its own laws. What are those laws? How do they operate? Feuerbach omitted to answer these fundamental questions. Man explained everything, but the man himself remained unexplained, and appeared as an absolute category.

Marx and Engels took up the thread at this critical point. They replaced Feuerbach's abstract conception of man by the dynamic conception of a social being—a factor involved in a process of continuous change. The basic principles of materialism were corrected and amplified by them, and re-stated in the following unambiguous form: "It is not the consciousness of men which determines existence; but on the contrary, it is their social existence which determines their consciousness." The consciousness of man is, indeed, determined by his physical existence; but the evolution of human thought—the spiritual progress of man,—is determined by social conditions which, in their turn, change the conditions of the physical being of man. The view that man is an absolute standard irresistibly leads to the conclusion that man must think similarly in all ages, under all circumstances. The next corollary to this absolutist conception would be the surprising reappearance of the ghost of the Eternal Truth and immutable standards of morality. Religion and metaphysics would re-enter furtively by the backdoor. The definition of man as a social being precludes the possibility of such deviations which are utterly irreconcilable with materialism.

All possible ambiguity about the "being" of man, which determines his consciousness, is definitely removed by the following view of man's relation to nature: "By acting on nature, outside himself, and transforming it, man simultaneously changes his own nature." (Karl Marx). The physical being of man is not a constant category. It implies an inseparable, eternal, relation with nature, man himself being a part of nature; and this relation—the most vital fact of man's being—is not a relation of passive contemplation, but of action which, therefore, is the essence of his being and as such determines his consciousness. The struggle for freedom from the ruthlessness of nature, as against the struggle for existence through adaptation, separates man from the lower animals. That struggle, in its turn, is undertaken by man not singly, but collectively. From his very birth (anthropologically), man is a social being. Therefore, the laws governing man's being are to be sought in his social relations, that is, in the terms and conditions on which human beings live together.

Aided by the discoveries of the natural sciences as well as by the Hegelian dialectic method of reasoning, Marx made an exhaustive investigation in the field of social history, and established the fact that the consciousness of man, after all, is determined "by the way he makes his living". Since man's modes of making his living (and the modes of living itself) change from time to time, the forms of his thought and the modes of expressing it change correspondingly. Religion, philosophy, ethics, aesthetics, law—all are but the variegated forms of an ideological super-structure raised upon the foundation of economic relations among distinct groups of individuals constituting a social aggregate.

"The great fundamental question of all philosophies," as Engels stated the proposition, "is connected with the relation between thought and existence, between spirit and nature." His answer to this fundamental question of philosophy is very definite:

"Materialism regards nature as primary, and spirit as secondary." Having clearly and concisely stated the basic principle of materialism, Engels raises questions concerning the theory of cognition: "The question of the relationship of thinking and being has another side. In what relation do our thoughts, with regard to the world surrounding us, stand to the world itself? Is our thought in a position to recognise the real world? Can we, in our ideas and notions of the real world, produce a correct reflection of the reality?"* The answer to these fundamental questions of epistemology differentiates the two contending systems of philosophy, namely, materialism and idealism, the latter being, as characterised by Feuerbach, "philosophical spiritualism".

The idealist doctrine that a mysterious gulf separates, for ever, the phenomenal world from the "world in itself" is nothing but the familiar religio-theological juxta-position of spirit and matter, soul and body; God and nature, as thesis and antithesis, as freedom and bondage, as reality and illusion. "It is an abyss", to quote Feuerbach once again, "created by the priests and adopted by the professors of philosophy." Materialism does not recognise this unbridgeable gulf, and experimental science has demonstrated beyond a shadow of doubt that no such gulf exists except in the fantasy of "philosophical spiritualism"..

Pantheistic mysticism or mystic pantheism, the outstanding feature of Indian philosophy, asserts that one can cross the Rubicon and taste the bliss of real knowledge on the other side; but the assertion

* Engels "Feuerbach: The Outcome of Classical Philosophy."

loses all force, except that of idle dogmatism, when it is associated with the admission that returning from that land of dream, none can describe what he has seen there: "Religious experience" is not communicable. Again the same old story: You must fall back upon faith, and believe in the "seer". His inexplicable dreams, fever-fantasies, trances, which may not seldom be sheer imposture, should be accepted as infallible, inspired wisdom—an effulgent ray of the divine light—as against the demonstrable knowledge of experimental science. This is denial of objective truth, the cognisability of which is the cardinal principle of materialism. To make of truth a purely subjective category, existing only in the dreams and fantasies of individuals, is to rule out truth as a reality. And that monstrosity is committed by the opponents of materialism.

On the basis of the successive stages of the development of modern materialistic epistemology, a basis subsequently rendered unshakable by the discoveries of natural sciences, Marx and Engels built up the complete and comprehensive structure of historical materialism. The fundamental epistemological principle of Marxian materialism are the following: "1. Things exist independently of our consciousness, independently of our sensations; 2. There is absolutely no difference between a phenomenon and the thing in itself, and there can be none. The difference is only between what is already known and what is yet unknown; 3. In the theory of knowledge, as in other branches of science, we must think dialectically, that is, we must not regard our knowledge as ready-made and unchangeable, but must determine how from ignorance knowledge is gradually built up, and how incomplete and inexact knowledge becomes more complete and more exact."*

The means to knowledge is action, not passive contemplation. As an object of passive contemplation, the nature would always remain an unfathomable mystery. Whether the senses supply us with true pictures of outside objects, can be ascertained only by going out of ourselves, by reaching out to the objects and comparing them with our perceptions of them. The taste of the pudding is in eating. The "thing-in-itself" ceases to be unknowable, becomes fully and positively known, as soon as we make it a thing-for-us. Nor is this approach to nature a new departure. Man's relation with nature has been from the very beginning not of passive contemplation, but of action. When the primitive man gathered fruit from the tree or caught fish from the river, and ate them to satisfy his hunger, he acquired definite knowledge about the things called fruit and fish. No amount of philosophical hair-splitting could ever persuade him to believe that the "fruit-in-itself" or the "fish-in-itself" might be something different from the images they made on his retina. The act of eating, and the result of that act—satisfaction of hunger—were fully convincing. Let a Berkeley or a Sankaracharya try to teach the man, consciously standing in the relation of activity to nature, that the fruit he eats is an illusion, that the fish is a fantasy; he would simply laugh the wise man out of court.

* Lenin, "Materialism and Empirio-Criticism".

Man's relation to nature has always remained one of action, but "spiritual" civilisation, that is, the rise of religion, theology, religious philosophy and metaphysics, made him forget the real essence of his being. Just as, by virtue of his ever-increasing activity, man's knowledge of nature increased correspondingly, he was taught the blessed doctrine of ignorance: Ideas are not the abstraction of his activities; they exist by themselves, inspiring his activities. Practice, the very basis of life, was totally divorced from the theory of life. The theory of life was not to be derived from, and verified by, the practice of life. The theory of life was a matter of divine inspiration—a mysterious, but imperative voice from "the other side" where the mind of man cannot penetrate. The theory of life, which should dictate the practice of life, was thus made entirely independent of the latter. Sensual knowledge, that is, the real knowledge acquired by man in course of his action upon nature, was branded as an illusion, at the best, an inferior sort of knowledge which is of no value for solving the "profound" metaphysical problems of life.

The root-cause of this absurd confusion, as a matter of fact, falsification, in the realm of epistemology, was unearthed by Marx and Engels. "From that moment, (when the theory of life is separated from the practice of life, through the division of labour into spiritual and material), consciousness may in reality imagine that it is something other than the consciousness of existing things. From the moment that consciousness begins really to imagine something, without imagining something real, from that time onward it finds itself in a position to emancipate itself from the world, and proceed to the formation of phantoms as basic elements of knowledge, —absolute categories of truth, eternal—and immutable."*

The phenomenal progress of the natural sciences in the nineteenth century exposed the utter absurdity of the "spiritualist" doctrine of epistemology which had condemned man to eternal ignorance, and proclaimed the real world an illusion. Neither science nor philosophical materialism claims absolute knowledge. That is the stock-in-trade of the religionists, modern as well as ancient, Eastern as well as Western. Only by rejecting the dogma of absolute knowledge, can we appreciate knowledge in its native spiritual dignity and sublimeness. Only then does human spirit appear in the perspective of infinity. Science does not put forward the stupid claim that it knows everything. That would be tantamount to the hymn at the funeral of humanity. For, if everything is known, there will be nothing more to do, and life will automatically come to an end. What science has proved, is that there is nothing unknowable; and materialist philosophy adds the corollary that, whatever is within the ken of human consciousness is material. Because, something immaterial (spiritual, in the traditional sense) can never be cognisable to human mind, itself a product of matter in a particular state of organisation. Science visualises, *in reality*, what religion and metaphysics have only idly imagined, namely, the omni-

* Marx, "Thesis on Feuerbach."

potence and omniscience of human soul—not in space, but in time. Omnipotence and omniscience, to be real, must be seen in a process—in terms of time. The materialist theory of knowledge endows human spirit even with the attribute of immortality; the consciousness of the man of a given epoch is the embodiment of knowledge accumulated in the past, and will continue to live in the endless progress of knowledge in the future. The materialist theory of knowledge can be summarised as follows.

Sense-perceptions, human experience, gained not in passive contemplation (it cannot be done that way), but in active functioning of the human organism, and having for their source the material world existing objectively outside our consciousness, independent of it, is the point of departure of all knowledge. There is no end to the process of acquiring such knowledge; the more we know, further there will be to know; and since every step forward in the process of enlightenment corrects, adds to, amplifies our previous stock of knowledge, there is no such thing as perfect knowledge or ábsolute truth.

The natural philosophers of the eighteenth and nineteenth centuries, though hindered by their poetical imagination from taking a strictly scientific attitude, nevertheless stood on the ground of materialism inasmuch as most of them held the activist theory of life. Goethe, for example, wrote: "I should not know what to do with eternal beatitude, unless it would offer me new tasks and difficulties to be conquered. But they will be provided. We need only look at the planets and the sun; there we shall also have nuts to crack."* Lessing also said the same thing in different words: "If the Almighty offered me the choice between truth and the search for the truth, I would unhesitatingly take the latter." Here we have the spirit of philosophic materialism breathed by poetic geniuses whose works will ever remain among the most beautiful specimens of the creation of human spirit.

The activist essence of philosophical materialism is set forth in the following thesis: "The question if objective truth is possible to human thought is not a theoretical, but a practical question. In practice, man must prove the truth, that is, the reality and force, and the this-sidedness of his thought. The dispute as to the reality or unreality of thought, which is separated from practice, is a purely scholastic question." †

The world of pure thought, that is, the world of spirit, is not separated from the sensual world, from the world of phenomena, by an unscalable wall. Pure thought is not of transcendental origin. There is no "other side" in contrast to "this side"; there is no world of spirit beyond the world of matter; no world of reality as against the world of illusion; no world of self-effulgent truth, distinct from the world of confusing half-truths; no world of sublime beatitude, counter-posed to the world of baffling and bewitching twilight of sense-perceptions. Pure thought, that is, spiritual activity of man, is the abstraction of activities constituting the basis of his material

* "Letters."

† Marx, "Thesis on Feuerbach."

being. Faith, religion, mysticism—all these old prejudices are the progeny of ignorance.

The declaration of pseudo-scientific scepticism, agnosticism and modern idealistic philosophy, that we do not and cannot know more of the external world than its reflection upon our senses, that objective truth is beyond our reach, leaves the way open for the old prejudices to creep in to cramp human spirit. Since "scientific" thinkers themselves admit the inability of sensual knowledge to include the whole truth of the universal being, who is there to dispute the claims of the advocates of revelation, inspiration and religious experience?

This question naturally arises if we take the oracle of the pseudo-scientific mystics as decisive. But the natural sciences do not allow us to take their idealist wisdom for granted. Objective truth, that is, the truth about the Universe as it exists by itself, outside of our sense-perception, is no longer an illusive category. The natural sciences have proved that it is knowable, the evidence being that we know more and more every day. Once it is established theoretically, not on the basis of speculation, but of human practice, that for explaining the Universe, there is no necessity for assuming a Noumenon behind phenomena, that the Universe itself contains all the data for its explanation, offers us the key to the endless knowledge of its being, the dealers in divine wisdom, spiritual inspiration and occult knowledge find it difficult to vend their glittering trinkets. That has been done by Marxian materialism which rests, in addition to the corner-stone of materialist thought, developing ever since the days of Democritos, on the twin-pillars of scientific knowledge and dialectic logic.

Lately, the opponents of materialism have been jubilant with the imagination that a powerful weapon has acceded to them from the most unexpected quarter, namely, physics. In the introduction to the English edition of Lange's "History of Materialism", Bertrand Russell, for example, writes: "The theory of relativity, by merging time into space-time, has damaged the traditional notion of substance more than all arguments of philosophers. Matter, for common-sense, is something which persists in time, and moves in space. But for modern relativity-physics, this view is no longer tenable. A piece of matter has become, not a persistent thing with varying states, but a series of inter-related events. The old solidity is gone, and with it the characteristics that, to the materialist, made matter seem more real than fleeting thoughts. Nothing is permanent, nothing endures; the prejudice that the real is the persistent must be abandoned."

If materialism could be demolished through the refutation of what it does not maintain, then, it should succumb to attacks like this. The theory of relativity might go against the "common-sense" view of matter, but its negation of the scientific basis of materialist philosophy is rather the product of desire of the impotent opponents of the latter than a fact. Indeed, the conclusion that "nothing is permanent, nothing endures" is only a corroboration of the dialectic logic of materialism. It is really surprising that a scientist like Bertrand Russell should know so little of materialism as to take one of its cardinal principles for a decisive argument against it. The conception of time merging itself into space, and becoming space-time, if it were really antagonistic to materialism, could be used not against it as such, but only to refute its dialectic method. It could be a weapon against the eighteenth century French materialism, or the German naturwissenschaftlichen Materialismus (nature philosophy) of the last century, expounded by Buechner, Moleschot, Vogt etc. Both those earlier schools of materialism were vitiated by the lack of a historical sense. By reviving the ancient dialectical method of thought, Hegel helped materialism to shake off its last limitation. The ancient materialism also did not suffer from a static view of things. It was inseparably associated with dialectic logic. Therefore, for the modern dialectic materialism, the theory of relativity is not a negation, but a positive accession of strength.

The conception of time is inseparably associated with the idea of evolution. It would be very unlikely for the theory of relativity to dispute the evolutionary nature of things, for the honour of being a handmaiden to idealism. The theory of relativity presages a higher stage of scientific knowledge. This it cannot conceivably do by knocking off the very bottom of modern science. Besides, the conception of movement in space without time can be traced to Hegel whose absolute idea expresses itself all at once in nature—not in time, but only in space. This queer, altogether anti-scientific (one might even say, anti-Hegelian) conception is in crass contradiction to the Hegelian method of thought, which was based upon the accumulated experience of mankind. Historical materialism, expounded by Marx and Engels, thoroughly exposes the impossibility of things happening not in time, but in space only. It was done with Hegel's own dialectic method, freed from Hegelian idealism. Hegel set up the palpably impossible theory in order to establish the priority of absolute idea. The theory of relativity has no such axe to grind. Therefore, its conception of space-time is entirely different from the Hegelian fantasy of evolution in space, but not in time. One represents a closer acquaintance with the objective reality of things, whereas the other was a view, subjectively expounded for rounding up a system of speculative philosophy. The space-time conception of the theory of relativity is another step in advance towards materialistic monism.

Yet, the age-long idealist tradition of human culture dies hard. Whenever human mind begins to penetrate unknown regions, idealistic prejudices are likely to creep in, because at that moment it is steeped in ignorance about the new field of investigation, notwithstanding all the knowledge that it already possesses. But at such points of transition, theories, established by previous experience, serve as reliable guides, and as guarantee against deviations.

Ever since Henri Poincare dramatically declared that physical theories were overtaken by a "crisis", theoretical (mathematical) physics has been providing hope to idealist philosophy. The differential equations of Hertz and Maxwell, when first formulated as a convenient method of stating physical conceptions, were eagerly welcomed as a "conclusive refutation" of materialism. It was held that the system of equation dispenses with the concept of matter; there was no objective reality, physics only dealt with symbols. Of course, mathematicians are sometimes carried away by their system of calculation, forgetting in their theoretical abstraction that something is being calculated. Two apples added to another two make four apples. The arithmetical axiom $2+2=4$ is taught and learned as a pure theoretical concept. But always the numbers stand for something concrete. If any schoolboy would take it into his head to dispute the correctness of the axiom, no mathematical genius will ever be able to convey conviction to the silly child theoretically. The mathematician, should he care to defend the prestige of his axiom, must get down from the altitude of his abstraction, and busy himself with the vulgar concrete of so and so many apples or something else equally concrete. Exactly similar is the case with the more abstract differential equations. They are not mere symbols, but are the convenient method of dealing with objective realities.

Nevertheless, it is a fact that the danger of idealist deviation is inherent in the pure abstractions of higher mathematics; but the danger is overcome by the experimental branch of physics. In the case of Hertz and Maxwell, the balance was kept by the great German physicist Boltzmann. He combated the attempt to utilise mathematical physics as a support for idealist philosophy. Replying to the "Symbolists" and "Phenomenologists", he said: "Those who propose to eliminate atomism by means of differential equations, cannot see the wood for the trees.

If we do not wish to entertain any illusion about the significance of the differential equations, there can be no doubt that this picture of the world (presented by the equations) must necessarily be in essence atomic; that is, it will be a summary description that, in accordance with certain rules, larger quantities of objects situated in a three-dimensioned space will be conceived as changing in time."

Hertz and Maxwell themselves also were far from the danger of constructing an idealist philosophy on the basis of their equations. They declared that the equations, that is, purely mathematical abstractions, did not preclude the construction of a mechanical theory of electricity out of real elements.

Just as the earlier mathematical theories, the theories of "new physics" of our days also may bring a ray of hope to the defenders of a lost cause; but just as in the past, in the present also, the hope is being rudely shattered by the advance in the experimental branch of physics. In short, the whole confusion arises from the idealistic prejudice of regarding mathematics as an independent science which does nothing more than express abstract concepts in figures. In reality, mathematics is an instrument of experimental science—a sort of short-hand of science. The mistake made by a short-hand reporter does not portray a mental defect of the speaker.

Developing within the framework of the bourgeois society, science, if isolated from the general, all-embracing philosophical synthesis, is apt to lend, often unconsciously, support to idealism, indeed, even to teleology and anthropomorphic religion. The likelihood becomes all the greater in proportion as bourgeois society decays. But it is idle for the opponents of materialism to expect such support from a physical conception which is associated with it from a very early stage of development.

The Epicureans visualised time merging into space. Of course, owing to the backward objective conditions, they could not do so with any degree of mathematical precision or experimental exactitude. Nevertheless, the conception is not altogether new; far from being a negation of materialism, it originated as an integral part of the mechanistic-physical view of the Universe.

Matter survived the "crisis" already a generation ago. None would to-day dispute the reality of the atom, now that it is actually being hammered in the laboratory to give out vast stores of energy to be used for practical purposes. To-day the objective reality portrayed by the concept of matter is too well recognised to be shaken by any pseudo-mathematical jugglery. What, after all, did the famous "crisis" of physical theories really mean? In the last analysis, it involved the *conception* of matter; it did not affect the existence of matter as such. The controversy centred upon the nature of matter, the existence of which itself, in some form or other, was not contested by any scientist of authority. The "crisis" simply exposed the inadequacy of the old atomist theory. It simply showed that the atom was not the ultimate, irreducible, state of matter. The substance of the "crisis" was that it appeared to reduce matter from mass to energy or radiation. There was nothing particularly new in that changed conception of the nature of matter, which could turn over all the traditional theories of physics and mechanics. From the days of Democritos, materialists always visualised the substratum of the Universe as matter-in-motion. They never conceived matter and motion as two distinct entities. Motion is a property of matter. Years before the "crisis", Engels conceived motion as a "form of material being". Therefore, the new physical theories do not amount to anything but a greater, closer, more concrete, knowledge of matter.

Another result of the "crisis"—a corollary to the supposed disappearance of matter—was considered by "philosophers" to be the destruction of the old theory of mechanics. In the absence of mass, all the traditional laws of mechanics become untenable. Physics appeared to abolish the mechanistic conception of the Universe, and provide proof for the re-establishment of teleology.

That the crisis did not spell disaster for science and materialist philosophy is testified by the fact that the traditional theories of physics still counted among their supporters such great names as Kirchhof, Hertz, Maxwell, Boltzmann, Helmholtz, Kelvin, Lorentz, Larmor, Langevin and many others. Even the "Positivists" admitted that the "crisis", after all, was but a milestone on the road of the development of physical theories. Assuming that the then hypothetical laws of electro-magnetism would lead to a modification of the traditional law of mechanics, one of them raises the question: "Would it signify the abandonment of mechanism?"

His answer is clear enough: "By no means. The pure mechanistic tradition would continue to persevere, and mechanism would follow its normal course of development."* The Positivist historian of the "crisis" then continues: "Matter is reduced to electrical particles, the ultimate elements of the atom. Motion, as displacement in space, remains a uniquely typical element in physical theory. And finally, from the viewpoint of the general spirit of the science of physics,—its methods, its theories and their relation to experience—physics remains absolutely identical with the view of mechanism which was ushered in with the Renaissance."

Turning to the co-related proposition of motion without matter, equally decisive and more authoritative opinions are found against it. "The real reason why physics at present prefers to express itself in terms of energy is that in this way it best avoids talking about things it knows very little of. It is true that we are now convinced that ponderable matter consists of atoms; and we have definite notions of the magnitude of these atoms, and of their motion in certain cases. But the form of the atoms, their motions in most cases—all these are entirely hidden from us. So that, although our conception of atoms is an important and interesting object of further investigation, it is in no wise specially fit to serve as a known and secure foundation for mathematical theories." † It is clear from this statement that Hertz's doubt was not about ponderable matter itself, but about its construction. Such

* A. Rey, "Contemporary Physical Theories."
† Heinrich Hertz, "Works."

doubt is in the nature of science. Without it, science would cease to be science, and degenerate into a body of dead dogmas. The spirit of enquiry is the lever of scientific progress which adds constantly to the knowledge of man. Hertz's doubt about the construction of ponderable matter only led towards the conception of "motion as a form of matter". One of the founders of dialectic materialism had the conception philosophically years before it found an empirical basis. Then, physicists prefer to talk in the terms of energy, not as the substitute for ponderable matter; but simply because of its being more accurately known, one could speak in terms of energy with greater precision. At that moment, the knowledge of the motion happened to be more precise than that of the things moving. There was absolutely no doubt that there was something moving; otherwise, there would be no motion.

W. Waubel, the author of standard works on physical chemistry, proves that the latest discoveries (radium, electron etc.) helped to form a more concrete idea about the nature of atoms and molecules, and the forces acting between and within them. He decisively rejects the proposition of motion without matter. He holds that motion presupposes the existence of matter. The very definition of motion, as displacement in space, implies the existence of something moving. If the mass is merged in motion, then motion becomes a form of matter. In his book on electricity, Waubel sets forth the view that electrical phenomena are produced by the motion and interaction of electrons which are particles of atoms. This view has since been indisputably borne out by the latest discoveries about the internal state of atoms. For example, in the beginning of 1932, Professor Chadwick of Cambridge discovered what has been named the "neutron". It is a close combination of proton and electron, so tightly bound together that it has no electric charge. This discovery definitely proves the fact that electricity is a form of matter. It is not pure motion, but mass-in-motion.

All scientists, without any metaphysical preoccupation, find in the electric theory of matter only another step forward towards the knowledge of the unitary basis of the Universe. "Every purely kinetic conception of nature means nothing but that there are a certain number of moving objects: these may be called electrons or something else."* The universal phenomena cannot be conceived kinetically, that is, in the terms of energy, without the presupposition of a mass, however fine that might be. Electrical particles, particles of energy, are material entities. The concept of electron does not do away with mass. It represents a closer knowledge of the construction and movement of matter.

The French physicist Cornu wrote: "The more we conceive the phenomena of nature, the more develpoed and precise becomes the brave Cartesian view of the world—mechanism: In the physical world, there is nothing save matter and motion. The problem of the unity of the various physical forces has again been put into the background after the great discoveries made at the end of the nineteenth century. The attention of our modern leaders of

* E. Becher. "Phylosophical Presuppositions of the Exact Natural Sciences."

science—Faraday, Maxwell, Hertz—was chiefly concerned with defining nature more accurately through new hypotheses about the properties of ponderable matter which is the vehicle of the world-energy." A return to the Cartesian view of world-mechanism does not mean the destruction of the traditional doctrines of physics by its new theories. Nearly a decade later, the famous English chemist William Ramsay wrote: "One so-called element can no longer be regarded as ultimate matter; but it is itself undergoing change into a simpler form of matter. Now it is almost certain that negative electricity is a particular form of matter; and positive electricity is matter deprived of negative electricity—that is, minus the electric matter. Now, what is electricity? It used to be believed formerly that there were two kinds of electricity, one called positive and the other negative. At that time, it would not have been possible to answer the question. But recent researches make it probable that what used to be called negative electricity is really a substance. Indeed, the relative weight of its particles has been measured. Atoms of electricity are named electrons."*

So, the electron is not a mysterious entity. It does not destroy the conception of mass. It has a mass itself. Energy is not an immaterial entity. It is a form of matter. The new theories do not destroy the mechanistic conception of the Universe. They do not visualise motion without matter. Matter is not "dematerialised". On closer acquaintance, it yields more of its secrets for the knowledge of man. What has previously been believed to be

* "Chemical Essays."

its absolute attributes, turns out to be relative—properties of matter in a certain state. Atom has not disappeared. The old conception of it has been modified in the light of a greater knowledge about it. The atom has disappeared as the basic unit of matter. It has been discovered to be a minute solar system, composed of a large number of infinitesimally small particles of matter.

Having survived the "crisis" which overtook it in the beginning of the century, physics has gone through yet another period of tremendous progress. While the theory of relativity has revolutionised it in the macrocosmic aspect, the same has been done by the development of the Quantum Theory in the microcosmic sphere. An entirely new department has been opened,—the atomic physics. The investigation into the atomic mechanism is still incomplete. Naturally, they are outstanding problems for physics. They are again hailed by the incorrigible opponents of materialism as the signs of yet another "crisis". But the questions raised to-day are of purely epistemological nature. The answer to them can be given only in the light of the relation between physics and psychology. The advance of biological knowledge, on the other hand, has thrown much light on that solution which to-day does not appear to be very distant. In the last analysis, epistemological problems are psychological problems. The present confusion regarding the ontological reach of the theories of new physics results from approaching physical problems from the psychological point of view. As regards the substance and structure of the world, there is, however, no room for any serious scientific doubt. Even the electron has been traced down to a state where particles disappear. To-day the substratum of the world has been revealed to be an all-pervasive substance. That is the philosophical implication of the "wave theory" of matter. The dualist conceptions of mass and motion, matter and energy have become untenable. The world has been analysed down to a unitary substance. Not only matter can be converted into energy, but energy also can be converted into matter. That has been demonstrated experimentally. So, energy is a material entity. That being the case, the fact that the substratum of the world is composed of waves of energy does not prove that the world is made of a spiritual substance. Physics thus has vindicated materialism, having provided it with an unshakable foundation of positive knowledge.

# CHAPTER VI

## MATERIALISM AND PRACTICAL IDEALISM

MATERIALISM is the philosophy of revolution. Revolutions are inherent in the process of human development. Therefore, materialist philosophy is a necessity in all ages. Its revolutionary essence, brought out in sharp relief by Marx and Engels, distinguishes it from other modes of thought. According to it, knowledge is derived not in passive contemplation, but in action. "Philosohers have interpreted the world in various ways, but the real task is to transform it."* Only in the process of transforming the world continuously, does the store of human knowledge endlessly increase; and the knowledge of a given epoch is valuable in so far as it enables man to transform the world, thereby opening a new epoch of progress.

Hegel declared change to be the only reality. "Everything that is, is real." This view makes a revolution in the conception of the history of mankind,—spiritual as well as material. History is seen in a process of continuous changes, each stage of which is as real as the other, and as realities all the stages are necessary, that is to say, determined. Thus, in spite of Hegel's idealism, idea ceases to be absolute. His dialectics destroyed absolute idealism. All that remained to be done was to bring it down on earth, and find its root in the process of material changes.

* Marx and Engels, "Thesis on Feuerbach.".

A Hegelian in his youth, Marx rescued the positive element of Hegelian philosophy—dialectic logic—out of its "fever fantasies", and employed it in the elaboration of materialism. He "set Hegelian philosophy on its feet".

"In its mystic form, dialectics became the fashion in Germany, because it seemed to elucidate the existing state of things. In its rational form, it is a scandal, and an abomination to the bourgeoisie and its doctrinaire spokesmen; because, while supplying a positive understanding of the existing order of things, it at the same time furnishes the understanding of negation of that state of things, and enables us to recognise that that state of things will inevitably break up. It is an abomination to them (bourgeoisie), because it regards every historically developed social form as in fluid movement, as transitory—because it is revolutionary." (Marx).

Materialism is not satisfied with contemplating what exists. It investigates the existing with the object of finding in it the cause of its destruction and the germs of a future, higher state of existence. It categorically rejects the shameful doctrine of ignorance—that there is a limit to our ability to know, a doctrine which, however plausibly dressed up in the garb of pseudo-science, harbours all the traditional enemies of science and of the real spiritual freedom of man—God, faith, religion, metaphysical abstraction, mysticism, occultism, so on and so forth. The materialist theory of cognition is firmly based upon the discoveries of modern science as well as upon a critical examination of the experience of mankind ever since the days of its birth.

By destroying the doctrine of eternal ignorance, and proving that there is nothing beyond the reach of human mind, that super-sensual categories are pure myth, invented to fortify the privileged position of the ruling classes, materialism sets human spirit free. The freedom from the metaphysical conception of the absolute, immutable, categorical, liberates man from the fetters of the traditional, of the respect and awe for the established order of the world. There is nothing sacrosanct, nothing permanent, nothing eternal. To change is the nature of everything. "Change is the only thing permanent," as old Heraclitos taught. Materialist philosophy inspires man to change the world and himself in the process.

Another distinguishing feature of materialism is that it is not a closed system like all the other schools of philosophy. It is not a dogma. It is a method of approaching nature, history, society—in short, life as a whole, in all its diverse departments, to learn the truth about it progressively, but surely. Indeed, in a way, materialism liquidates philosophy (in the narrow, speculative sense), inasmuch as it declares that there cannot be a closed system of complete knowledge, that there cannot be an end to the process of acquiring knowledge. Thus, philosophy ceases to be the brain-child of this or that or the other individual, brought up exclusively to be the pet mistress of the ruling class; or of a spiritually gifted race inhabiting a certain part of the globe. It becomes the highest spiritual creation of the entire mankind—a mighty lever to greater activity and higher knowledge on the part of man. The mission of philosophy is thus identical with the mission of mankind.

Materialism, being the philosophy of revolution, cannot naturally be accepted by the privileged upper classes, either of the East or of the West. Because, the interests, power and privilege of those classes, whether the bourgeoisie or the landed aristocracy or the priestly class, are bound up with the established social order. Materialism, therefore, is detested and combated no less passionately by the defenders of the present social order of the West than by the militant protagonists of the decayed Indian culture.

Those who denounce Western civilisation as "materialistic" are not only ignorant of what is materialist philosophy, but are utterly ill-informed about the dominating thought-currents of a civilisation they criticise. Except, partially, in the seventeenth and eighteenth century, official Western philosophy, ever since the days of Plato, has always been predominantly idealistic, transcendental, metaphysical, religious, mystic, pantheistic; in short, anti-materialist. The philosophy of the contemporary age of "rampant materialism" is idealism, often thinly veiled in specious sophistry or deceptive nomenclatures to make religious atavism appear "scientific".

The Indian intellectuals, who are so fond of professing idealism as against the abomination of materialism, are equally ignorant about both. Just as materialist philosophy is ignorantly confounded with the vulgar cult of "eat, drink and be merry", just so is idealism regarded not as a school of philosophy, but practical conduct of life. Generally, idealism is identified with the virtue of dedicating life to an Ideal. The idealist philosophy, however, is quite different from what is called "idealism" in common parlance. Apart from their wider meanings, even etymologically, the two terms are quite distinct. The former is derived from the word "idea", whereas the latter, from "ideal". The so-called "practical idealism" has nothing to do with the idealist philosophy. It is not rejected by the materialists. Indeed, the philosophical materialist is the greatest practical idealist. Can there be a higher ideal than to rebuild the world into a befitting home for a free, enlightened, happy mankind with an endless perspective and possibility of progress opened before it?

And there is nothing in life which every convinced materialist would not willingly sacrifice to advance mankind even one step towards that goal. Who is a greater "idealist", in the practical sense,—the atheistic scientist who cheerfully risks his life, often to death, to discover the cure for a fatal disease, or the pious anchorite who withdraws himself into the shell of his ego to save his precious soul, or the self-satisfied individual seeking beatitude in religious experience? Who is sincere in his idealism? The revolutionary workingman, who heroically faces persecution, prosecution, starvation, even death, either on the gallows or on the barricade, for the cause of human freedom; or the comfortable bourgeois or his well-paid and muddle-headed spokesman who sanctimoniously talks about "high and noble ideals" of life which only cement the social system of slavery, poverty, ignorance, demoralisation and degeneration? The moralists and Mahatmas preach the virtue of "simple living and high thinking" as hypocritical defenders of the vulgar materialism of the upper classes who, notwithstanding the pious teachings of their spokesmen, live a life of luxury and think meanly, if at all. If they don't do so consciously, (which may often be the case), such is the practical force of their "noble and lofty idealism". Only associated with the materialist philosophy can practical idealism be sincere.

The materialist does not reject practical idealism. He alone practises it consistently, sincerely, whole-heartedly. With the spiritualist, of any hue or shade, Western or Eastern, religious or philosophical, it is sheer philistinism, covering the egoistic essence of his cult. The ideal of life is the motive force of the life of the materialist. It is inseparable from his life. It grows out of his view of life. It is a part of his own self. The materialist is a practical idealist, because he cannot possibly be otherwise without abandoning his philosophy. For him, practical idealism is not a virtue to be cultivated under duress; it is natural. Without an ideal, life appears to him meaningless—not worth living. He lives for an ideal, is "righteous and noble" like Epicuros, "because it is a pleasure to be so."

Russia is the only country where materialism has become the official philosophy. Were the popular notions on materialism true, then, Russia to-day would present a crazy carnival of sensuousness and moral degeneration, deplored by the sanctimonious spiritualist. But what is really the moral atmosphere in the land of materialism? Let a truthful spiritualist paint the picture: "Godlessness may be the creed of Communism, but certainly not lovelessness. Everywhere one finds ardent Communists willing to give their lives for a cause which they believe is worth dying for. They may be working under desperate hardships, they may be sent on dangerous missions, they may be members of shock-brigades in the factories, toiling long hours at miserable wages, but they glory in sacrifice. To them, it is a privilege and an honour actually to help to translate into life the ideal of justice for all the people."*

It is just the opposite with the spiritualists. They may be idealists in philosophy, in so far as they are able to look upon life philosophically; but practically, they can have high ideals and live up to them (that, too, only in their own imagination), only because they are compelled to do so by a force which is not in them and which is superior to their own humanness. The believers in the spiritual essence of man and in the priority of the spirit over matter do not trust man to be virtuous, noble, moral, that is, to live an ideal life, by himself! Thus, they debase their own God—ridicule their own philosophy. This is not an interpretation, but admission of the spiritualists themselves. Here are two typical examples—one from the West, and the other from the East.

Mazzini's "Duties of Man" is the handbook of practical idealism. It is one of the few fortunate

* Dr. Jerome Davis, Professor of Practical Philanthropy at the School of Divinity, Yale University, U.S.A.

fountains of Western wisdom at which Indian nationalists thirstily drink. Mazzini refused to have anything to do with the materialist Marx, although none championed the cause of national liberation more ardently than the latter. There was a deep philosophical difference involved. In the opinion of the prophet of bourgeois nationalism, man had only duties; he totally ignored the rights of man. The philosopher of nationalism evidently had not read such historical documents as the epoch-making book of Thomas Paine or the ringing "Declaration of Rights" of the French Revolution. They also raised the voice of the bourgeoisie; but then the bourgeoisie was a revolutionary class and professed a largely materialistic philosophy. As a revolutionary class, necessarily with a revolutionary outlook of life, at the time, the bourgeoisie fought for the "Rights of Man". Less than a century later, Mazzini's philosophy of freedom totally disregarded the rights of man, and placed before him only duties. This is a classical example of what is commonly understood and admired as "Idealism". As a matter of fact, it is a doctrine of slavery. Duty without right is servitude. Nevertheless, Mazzini stood on the ground of spiritualism. He wrote: "The idea of an intelligent first cause once destroyed, the existence of a moral law supreme over all men, and constituting an obligation—duty imposed upon all men, is destroyed with it." That was evidently an attack upon materialism. Spiritualism is thus found to have defended a doctrine of slavery in the name of freedom. Philosophically, Mazzini laid down the foundation of Fascism.

An Indian spiritual imperialist perhaps would not blush to own Mazzini's view as the echo of Indian philosophy. But we need not rely on inference. Here is the opinion of the generally acknowledged contemporary authority on Hindu philosophy: "Our moral experience is not highest. The religious experience transcends the moral. Moral life may presuppose an unfinished Universe, a finite God, and a doubtful struggle. But the moral life would lose its validity and meaning, and moral struggle its inspiration, without the religious assurance. Morality points itself to religion, where we feel the oneness of the Universe, and see all things in God. Only the religious conviction assures us of the triumphant of good."* Practical idealism is possible only under the compulsion of religion! Man cannot be moral, intelligently, by conviction. Only the cudgel of the gods can compel him to behave decently. And we shall only have to look at the face of Mother India, the moral and spiritual condition of her famished children, to realise what sort of a moral tone results from religion.

The development of modern science coincided with the rise of a new social force in Europe,—the class of traders, manufacturers and bankers, struggling to liberate themselves from feudal bondage. By repudiating the authority of orthodox religion and theology, science destroyed the ideological foundation of the feudal social order. Deprived of the spiritual justification, the rule of absolute monarchy and despotic nobility must go. The bour-

* Radhakrishnan, "The Reign of Religion in Contemporary Philosophy."

geoisie preached, and eventually asserted, the "sacred right of revolt"—in temporal as well as spiritual matters, and became the ruling power. In a changed situation, under a new relation of classes advantageous to themselves, their outlook changed. As an oppressed class, they had advocated revolution, ideological as well as political; in power, they became conservative.

Without an authority, there could be no domination of one class over the entire society; and an authority on earth cannot be firmly established unless backed, directly or indirectly, by some celestial or super-natural authority. So, faith and religion were rescued from their ruins. For the vulgar, the old discredited God, with all his threadbare paraphernalia, was again allowed to rule; but the intellectual elite had become too sophisticated to relapse into crude beliefs, severely shaken, if not thoroughly exploded, by science. For their edification, religion appeared in the new role of idealism: The untenable doctrine of a personal Creator was replaced by the fascinating fantasy of the Abstract; Transcendental Idea.

The brilliant critic of the Christian Church, the cynical Voltaire, himself became an advocate of the lost cause, and replied the atheism of other philosophers, with the following argument: "If there is no God, we must discover one. Give Bayle (the most outspoken and consistent atheist of the eighteenth century) five hundred peasants to rule, and he will immediately recognise the usefulness of religion." This is the most forceful argument against religion, advanced by its defenders themselves. It holds up God and religion in their true role.

If the selfish interest of the bourgeoisie came in conflict with the philosophical revolution, and sought to curb its progress, the future of mankind required its consumation. Therefore, it was impossible to resist the historical striving to appreciate properly the far-reaching theoretical value of scientific discoveries, in their entirety, with the object of weaving them into a comprehensive system of philosophy. In order to disown the materialistic tendencies of its birth, modern philosophy had launched upon the wild career of idealism which was raised to a giddy height by Hegel. In his eagerness to vindicate the basic principle of a true philosophy, namely, the unity of things, Hegel destroyed modern classical philosophy. Without a dualist conception of the Universe, idealist philosophy is not possible. A monist conception must be either materialistic or be lost in the inextricable wilderness of solipsism and nihilism. If the original unity is reduced to a spiritual existence, the phenomenal world must be declared to be a hallucination. For, matter can never evolve out of pure spirit, except with the intervention of omnipotence which knows no law. With the postulate of such an intervention, religion is restored to the throne of authority, and philosophy must accept a humble place at the foot of the throne.

Spirit cannot exist without subordinating itself to the limitations of space, in which case it would cease to be what it claims to be. In the age of science and positive knowledge, mankind cannot possibly believe that the grand process of the evolution of the Universe is a bad dream. Therefore, materialism must be its philosophy, should it have any philosophy worth the name.

In the middle of the nineteenth century, the lowered banner of philosophical revolution was raised again, this time by the ideologists of the toiling masses. The proletariat is not only an oppressed class, but, by its very nature, cannot free itself without freeing the entire society from all forms of class domination, which must assume some supernatural authority as its ideological basis and moral sanction. Therefore, the revolutionary outlook of science, which rejects all *a priori* authority, can be fully and clearly adopted only from the point of view of the toiling masses.

The new leaders of the revolution were equipped with a formidable weapon forged by the last and greatest idealist philosopher. It was the dialectic method of thought which ousted formal logic. Exposing the transitoriness of everything, and by visualising the constant conception of a new in the womb of the passing old, dialectics puts an end to all authority. No weapon could be more welcome to the oppressed masses.

Out of the magnificent ruins of Hegelian absolute idealism, Feuerbach rescued the positive contributions of the classical philosophy as the basis for the "Philosophy of the Future". With an Encyclopedic knowledge, Karl Marx and Friedrich Engels clearly and comprehensively stated the new outlook of the Universe, opened by the discoveries of science during the preceding two hundred years. In the bright light of the materialist outlook, the problems of nature, life, history and society appear devoid of all mystery, and man attains the full height of his power and glory, as the sole master of his own destiny.

Finis.